IT'S A
JUNGLE
IN THERE

Inspiring Lessons, Hard-Won Insights, and
Other Acts of Entrepreneurial Daring

Steven Schussler,
founder of the Rainforest Cafe

with Marvin Karlins

UNION SQUARE PRESS
An imprint of Sterling Publishing Co., Inc.

New York / London
www.sterlingpublishing.com

STERLING and the distinctive Sterling logo are registered trademarks of Sterling Publishing Co., Inc.

Library of Congress Cataloging-in-Publication Data Available

10   9   8   7   6   5

Published by Sterling Publishing Co., Inc.
387 Park Avenue South, New York, NY 10016
© 2010 by Steven Schussler
Distributed in Canada by Sterling Publishing
c/o Canadian Manda Group, 165 Dufferin Street
Toronto, Ontario, Canada M6K 3H6
Distributed in the United Kingdom by GMC Distribution Services
Castle Place, 166 High Street, Lewes, East Sussex, England BN7 1XU
Distributed in Australia by Capricorn Link (Australia) Pty. Ltd.
P.O. Box 704, Windsor, NSW 2756, Australia

Sterling ISBN 978-1-4027-6289-5

For information about custom editions, special sales, premium and corporate purchases, please contact Sterling Special Sales Department at 800-805-5489 or specialsales@sterlingpublishing.com.

To my family and friends who have so boldly shared my vision . . . your selfless devotion, camaraderie, shared passion and enthusiasm gave me the credibility and wisdom to accept nothing less than yes. I could not have done it without all my friends from the Walt Disney World Company (especially Bud Dare, Maribeth Bisienere, George Aguel, Joe Rohde, Wing Chao, Keith Bradford, and David Stofcik), Jimmy Rittenberg, Lyle Berman, Herb Simon, Mel Simon, Tilman Fertitta, Nasser Kazeminy, John Goodman, Dan Lowe, Steve Graham, Richard Tettamant, Jon Donahue, Brent Kroener, Ken Cooley, Brian Stone, Tim Myslajek, Norm Pink, Dr. Bob Goldman, David Siegel, and Paul Ridgeway.

To my team at Schussler Creative—how lucky I am to have such a talented and dedicated team. My parents, Gloria and Jules; my grandfather, Bill Botwinik; my brothers, Robert and John; and Sunhi Ryan.

To all of the gatekeepers and other hardworking everyday folk who shared my dreams, respected my out-of-the-box thinking and helped me get where I wanted to go.

CONTENTS

PREFACE

For the last fifteen years or so, I've given so many lectures, talks, and workshops about my theory of good business that I can't even count them. My lessons always focus on the five Ps of successful entrepreneurship that I have discovered through my own experiences: Personality, Product, Persistence, People, and Philanthropy. In my life, I've had so much good come out of employing these core strategies. I've launched my dream business, the Rainforest Cafe, and watched it grow from an idea everyone thought was crazy into a hugely successful international company. Not only have I made it as a businessman by sticking to what I believe in, I've been able to bring happiness to the millions of kids of all ages who visit my indoor rainforests each year in search of an adventurous dining experience.

At those talks I give on business success strategies, I've been getting the same question over and over for so long I can't remember: "Steve, where can I buy your book?" I'm a businessman by trade, and never thought of myself as an author, so this was something I'd laugh off. I'd leave my business card, figuring the best way to sell my business strategy was with myself—after all, look at the first P, Personality—and go on to my next engagement.

But finally it hit me like an anvil! Steve, I thought, you're not even listening to yourself in these talks! What's the second P? Product! One of my central strategies for turning the Rainforest Cafe into the enormous success it has become is to always anticipate customer needs and interests—it's absolutely essential to constantly be on the lookout for products or services people will buy (I talk more about this strategy in Chapter 9). Now here were my actual customers of life—my students, the people attending my lectures, and the inspired and aspiring entrepreneurs-to-be—actually *telling* me the product they wanted me to sell them! And all this time I'd been laughing it off because I hadn't thought of myself as an author.

Well, this just goes to show you that every day in the business world is a new opportunity to grow and learn. So here I am, writing my book—not only purely for the reasons of the business strategies I put forth in it, but also in hopes that you, the reader, will be inspired by my story. The truth is, I've just had an amazing time doing what I love and chasing after my own dreams. In the spirit of the third P, Persistence, I never gave up, no matter how unreachable everyone told me those dreams were, and I learned in the end that if you want it badly enough and fight hard enough for it, nothing is out of reach. The idea that I might inspire other people to chase after their own dreams is as exciting as watching my own come true.

Most of the things that I create are highly theatrical and energetic—most projects involve partnering with people who are high-energy entrepreneurs and business professionals. In writing this book, I have tried to capture the energy bounced around during my daily interactions, the thought processes that we create and live by, and my belief in always taking the high road.

My professional life has been a roller-coaster ride, but it's been a fun one. I have reinvented myself many times, which is evidenced by the fact that I'd held more than a dozen jobs before my sixteenth birthday. I can't stop taking on new projects, thinking of new innovations, and trying out new things that people have avoided trying because it looks too difficult or too wild: sometimes they're right, and my project comes to nothing, but sometimes they're wrong and I strike upon something truly exciting. I found that the more I create, the happier I am. The happier I am, the more I create. The two go hand in hand.

Since this book is the story of a guy who's spent that whole roller-coaster ride trying to have fun, I believe that reading it will make you laugh. *It's a Jungle in There* was written to share the entrepreneurial stories from my career that I believe you will find motivational, educational, and serve as examples of real ways to connect with others that share the same out-of-the-box way of thinking. I share insights on how I look at problems and opportunities that have been everyday occurrences. I believe that I think differently. I have embraced and documented some of those thought processes with the goal of influencing you to *never give up—no matter what!*

Let me give you an idea of some of the key ideas I'm going to explore in *It's a Jungle in There.* First and foremost is *thank you.* One of the most important lessons I've learned in my entire life is to give credit where credit is due—the fact is, people may work for money, but they live for acknowledgment. By remembering to thank the people who have offered you their time and energy, you make lifelong allies. There are many people who have influenced me. You will hear about some of them throughout the book. I have tried to make certain that those who have touched my life in a significant way were included in the acknowledgments. If I have inadvertently left someone out, I apologize.

The second tenet of business life is taking the high road. My team and I have made a big deal in the book—and in life—about always taking the high road and about giving back. Both of these traits make you a better person and certainly a more successful entrepreneur.

A third key idea is tirelessness—you must keep trying. I use this example when I talk about frequency and consistency in pursuing your goals. When searching for a job, searching for a product, or searching for a solution to a problem, just remember that the more ships leave the port and go out to fight the war, the more ships return to port. So get out there. Don't send one résumé, send 150. Make sure that there are phone calls and follow-up letters. You just need to do a little bit more and a little bit better than everyone else in order to be extremely successful.

Fourth is attention to detail, one of the single most important aspects in anything you do. I am known as the "lightbulb nut." I believe lighting is jewelry in our everyday life: our office, our restaurants, my home . . . I cannot stand seeing a lightbulb out. Like a famous hotelier, I consider it a measure of attention to detail. If the lightbulb was so obvious, then what else is wrong?

I find myself quite often going into a restaurant, retail store, or business and focusing on the easy fixes I see that no one else would deem important. Sometimes it is subliminal—your guest or customer might not consciously see it but they feel it! As an entrepreneur, you can make sure you stand out from your competition by never letting the lightbulbs go out.

I can be demanding and loud, but I always try to add humor, and I am always thanking those around me. I am lucky to have such quality family and friends and such a great team. I am truly blessed.

As a final note, know that your purchase of this book has an even greater benefit than whatever you get out of the read. I am a founding board member and lifetime member of the advisory board of Smile Network International. The founder, Kim Valentini, is the true hero of this amazing nonprofit organization. Giving back is something that is the obligation of every entrepreneur. There are many ways to give back. Smile Network International (www.smilenetwork.org) and sharing my stories with young entrepreneurs are two of the ways that I can contribute. A portion of my proceeds of this book will go to support both of these causes.

SECTION I
PERSONALITY

CHAPTER 1

The Role of Risk-taking in Entrepreneurial Success

"Only those who will risk going too far can possibly find out how far one can go."

—T. S. Eliot

Self-examination Question:
Many people prefer to play it safe when it comes to business matters. Are you willing to take risks in the pursuit of entrepreneurial success?

Let me tell you a story about risk-taking. When I was eighteen years old, I moved to Miami and got work climbing telephone poles and crawling through sewers as a lineman for Southern Bell Telephone Company. It was hard work for little pay and offered limited opportunities for advancement. When I learned I could make more money selling airtime for radio and television stations and build a future career for myself, I knew it was time for me to make a move. The problem was trying to secure a full-time position when I already had one: how could I find the time to call prospective employers and set up interviews?

It took me a few days to come up with a plan. I noticed that all my coworkers were "brown baggers," meaning that they brought their own food to the job site and would climb down the telephone poles during lunchtime to eat. That left me with a window of opportunity: when my colleagues climbed down the poles for lunch, I climbed up, tapping into the phone lines to arrange job interviews. More than once I had to think fast when a homeowner would pick up her phone and hear me on the line. When it happened I'd say, "Just checking your phone connection, ma'am," hoping the homeowner would accept my story and hang up before a prospective interviewer got wind of what was happening. One hundred percent of the time, she did.

I was able to set up a few appointments, and so I'd climb down the telephone pole at five o'clock and go to my interviews with the station managers. For five months, I went from one interview to the next. The story was always the same: prospective employers told me, "You're the next guy we're going to hire" . . . until I told them my age. Nobody wanted to hire someone so young. So I stopped mentioning my age unless I was specifically asked, and then I'd add a few years to the answer. I looked old for my age; I could have easily passed for a twenty-seven-year-old.

My new approach got positive responses, but still no firm job offers. Finally, I decided to take things into my own hands. I wasn't going to take "no" or "we're still considering you" for answers any longer. I was going to do something risky that would either get me hired on the spot or, as my roommate at the time warned, get me incarcerated. (In fact, when he heard my plan, he actually offered me $50 for bail money. "You'll need it if you try and pull *that* off," he warned.)

I wanted to do something so wild and crazy that no one who saw it would ever forget it. I figured the risk was worth it. I wanted to make an impression that had such impact a prospective employer would have no choice but to hire me. And I was convinced that if I could just get past the secretaries and into the boss's office, I could make a showing that would put me on the payroll.

Superman Strategies

Once I decided on my grand strategy to get a job, it took me two days to put my plan into action. The first thing I did was visit a container company, where I purchased a wooden barrel large enough to fit in. Then I went to a costume shop and paid for a Superman outfit, complete with blue tights, red shoes, a cape, and a big S to wear on my chest. My last stop was at the apartment of two friends who happened to be Miami-Dade police officers. I offered them $100 each to deliver me—tucked inside the barrel—to the office of the station manager where I wanted to work. "You have to be in uniform and use the police paddy wagon to make the delivery," I said, hoping they'd agree. They did.

That night I discussed my plan with my next-door neighbor. She was so concerned I'd get hungry while being transported in the barrel that she fixed me a lunch, comprised of a deli-quality salami sandwich, a pickle, and a can of Diet Coke, to take along on the trip.

The next morning, I put my plan into action. My two officer friends, in full uniform, came to my apartment, stuffed me and my lunch into the barrel, and nailed it shut. Then they took a dolly and loaded me into the police van for the trip across town.

It was just five minutes into the journey that I discovered I had made two grievous errors: one, I hadn't drilled air holes into the barrel, and oxygen was becoming an increasingly scarce commodity; two, I had forgotten how hot Miami can be when you're crammed into a small space and the temperature is registering triple digits. Before long, I was gasping for air and sweating like a pig and, to make matters worse, the salami sandwich was beginning to stink like a refrigerator full of spoiled food after a power outage. I prayed to God that I wouldn't die in a Superman costume crumpled in a crate; it wasn't the legacy I had imagined for myself.

By the time we finally reached our destination, I was surviving on pure adrenalin and a dogged determination to complete my mission. The cops loaded me on a dolly, wheeled me into Station Manager Don Hamlin's outer office at WGBS Radio, and gave the secretary our prearranged story that they had a shipment of expensive furniture from Mexico for her boss.

I had assumed Hamlin would be there. That was my near-fatal error. As it turned out, he was attending a board meeting with the company's top executives in a hotel across the street.

I couldn't hear anything while sealed inside the barrel, but, fortunately, my friends persisted. They told the secretary they couldn't leave the furniture without the boss's signature. They urged her to call him on the phone, which she finally agreed to do. I was told later the conversation went like this:

"Mr. Hamlin, we have two policemen here with some expensive furniture you ordered from Mexico. They can't leave until you sign for it in person."

"Are you crazy? I didn't order any furniture from Mexico. And I've got twenty board members here!"

"Well, what should I do?"

"I'm coming right over, and there better be an explanation for all this."

At this point, I'd probably lost ten pounds from sweating, I smelled like a dead animal, and a crowd was gathering. To make matters worse, the Diet Coke I was holding had exploded from the heat, hurtling foam, soda, and salami fragments over my hair, face, and costume.

A few agonizing minutes later, Don Hamlin, followed by his entire board of directors, marched into the office. "What the hell is this all about?" he shouted at my two friends as they pried the nails from the barrel and prepared to lift off the top.

At this point I was thinking, "This is either going to be the best or the worst day of my life." I was also thinking if I didn't get a breath of air in the next thirty seconds, it would be the *last* day of my life.

As the lid slid away from the barrel, I came flying out like a jack-in-the-box, gasping for air and wiping Coke and salami from my eyes. The stench from the barrel filled the room.

I smiled at everyone and said, "Hello, everybody, my name is Steve Schussler. I'm your new super salesman." Then I went around and shook each person's hand. The board members were in various stages of shock. Finally the oldest guy—he must have been eighty years old—pointed at me with his cane and said, "Son, you are the sickest person we've ever met. You're hired."

I know what some of you are thinking: "That Superman gambit was a *really* risky maneuver." And you'd be right. Anytime you play Superman-in-a-barrel, it involves risk. Fortunately, some of this risk can be reduced by better understanding how those affected by your actions will most likely react to them. In my case, I had the advantage of being interviewed twice by Don Hamlin—the radio station manager who eventually hired me—and had been able to determine that he had a sense of humor. That knowledge helped me formulate my plan. It was because I felt Don would appreciate an off-the-wall approach that I tried the Superman stunt in the first place.

There is a moral to my Superman story: If you want to be a successful entrepreneur, you have to be a risk-taker. Passion, ambition, and talent are all traits that help a businessperson make it to the top, as you need all three to work your way up the corporate totem pole. But you need guts to be in business for yourself.

A successful businessperson operating in a corporate environment is like an acrobat doing all kinds of elaborate tricks on a high wire. Sure, it's impressive, but he's got a safety harness on.

Where's the danger in that? Entrepreneurship is like performing a steady walk across two forty-foot-high platforms. It doesn't have to involve fancy footwork; it can be just moving gingerly along the taut wire strung forty feet above the arena floor. What makes the performance impressive is that lack of a safety net.

If you want to be a successful entrepreneur, you have to be a risk-taker. You can't worry about falling. There's no room for the faint of heart, for the risk-averse player, in the entrepreneurial game. When it comes to your career, there's a good chance you'll experience some bumps and bruises along the way, even some ego-crushing and wallet-flattening descents from high places. But there is great reward and satisfaction awaiting the entrepreneur who can handle risk, walk the wire between failure and success, and come out a winner on the other side.

Risky Business

I found out firsthand the risks inherent in starting your own business. It happened in Chicago when I was in my twenties. I had a good job selling television advertising. But there was a problem. One day, I calculated that I was making $4 to $5 million for the company but getting only 0.0085 percent back in commissions for my efforts. It didn't seem fair. I was working sixteen hours a day, creating a lot of wealth for someone else. I realized that I might do better if I was on my own.

At the same time I was questioning my pay (or lack of it), I happened to visit an antique shop where I spotted a broken-down, vintage Wurlitzer jukebox. It was one of the old, fancy art deco kinds, with lots of neon and bubbles flowing through translucent cylinders that bordered the front of the machine. The owner offered to sell it to me for $500. I told him it was wrecked, but that didn't faze him. "I'll tell you where you can get all the parts you need to fix it up," he told me. "Once you do that it'll be worth $5,000." Despite my doubts, I took him up on the offer.

It took me less than twenty-four hours to experience a severe case of buyer's remorse. The jukebox was more damaged than I'd originally thought, so I went back to the store to try and get a refund. The guy refused. I had no choice but to buy the parts and get the thing working.

It turned out I actually enjoyed doing the work to restore it. Then I turned around and sold the jukebox for $4,500! Considering that it only cost $1,000 for the parts, plus the original $500 I paid, I was showing a healthy profit—a far better return on my investment than I was receiving with my real job.

I became passionate about jukeboxes and other antiques, particularly old carousel horses and slot machines. I learned everything I could about their cost, worth, and history as collectables. I spent time repairing and restoring them, getting them into the kind of shape that would attract buyers and provide me with a nice profit margin. I became so convinced I had found a niche market that I figured I could turn my newfound hobby into a business.

I decided to rent a store where I could sell the nostalgia items I had restored and call it Juke Box Saturday Night. I found some commercial space and started moving things in. I assumed I'd be able to get everything up and running in a weekend, but it took longer than expected. As a result, I took off Monday as a sick day from work to finish things up.

It's hard to explain the excitement I felt when I heard my new business phone ring for the first time that Monday afternoon. Here I was, about to do business in my very own place. I was amazed: my listing in the yellow pages had yet to be published, the store wasn't listed in any directories, I hadn't done any advertising . . . and yet word must have gotten out that Juke Box was opening. What a start!

"Juke Box Saturday Night," I answered proudly. "Can I help you?"

Turns out I couldn't. Worse, it turned out that the caller was my TV sales manager who had found out about my business venture and unceremoniously fired me on the spot. Now that I was out of a job, I was truly an entrepreneur. I had taken a risk and now I felt like the ground had just caved in. I had no income and I'd just taken out a $100,000 loan against my condo.

Things went downhill from there. People loved my store, and they'd stop in and admire the stuff like they were in a museum, but nobody bought anything. I had to file for bankruptcy. In lieu of foreclosure, I surrendered my condo and my company truck was repossessed. I was so poor I had to wear the same clothes for days in a row. I ended up living in a small nine-by-twelve-foot office above the dance floor of a place called the Rodeo Nightclub. I was jammed in with my inventory of antiques and my sheepdog, forced to listen to honky-tonk music until 4 a.m. every morning. That's when my dog went berserk and attacked me. I ended up in the hospital from the dog bites. I got so bored being confined to my bed that I made it my goal to come up with a hundred new ways to make my Juke Box Saturday Night name and idea a success.

One of those ideas panned out: I joined with the owner of

the Rodeo Nightclub, Jimmy Rittenberg, to develop a 1950s retro dance club, decorating it with the jukeboxes and other antiques from my defunct store. At least I got one thing out of the failed venture: we took the name of the store and called our new club and restaurant Juke Box Saturday Night.

The venture turned out to be a huge success. We opened four establishments in Chicago, and expanded to Des Moines; San Francisco; Springfield, Massachusetts; and Minneapolis. I ended up moving to Minneapolis to manage the Juke Box there. With the profits we were making, it felt like we were literally minting money. I felt great. My initial risk, trying to be an entrepreneur while holding down a regular job, was costly. I was fired, suffered economic hardship, and was even mauled by my own dog. But, in the long run, the risk was well worth it because it forced me to find a new way to make a living and gave me the opportunity to find my true calling in life. I became a creator of attractions, themed restaurants, and retail stores—a passion that occupies my mind and captures my heart to this day.

Risk-taking is, at least to me, part of what being an entrepreneur is all about. There are probably some successful risk-aversive businesspeople out there who would take issue with me, but, ultimately, I truly believe that if it's not worth the risk, it's probably not worth the reward.

CHAPTER 2

The Importance of Passion

"Passion makes perfect."

—EUGENE BIRO

Self-examination Question:
If you were independently wealthy and never had to work a day in your life, would you still choose to spend your time attempting to become a successful entrepreneur?

Back in the 1990s, a friend sent me a statement someone had written on the topic of passion. I use it as an introduction to all my speeches on entrepreneurship because it captures the essence of how important passion is for success in business and in life. It says, "Passion is the Engine of Success."

Passion is called by many names: drive, desire, hunger, and motivation. Passion is the power that is released to take action when someone feels intense about someone or something. As a leadership quality, one's own passion is what galvanizes others into action.

Of this I am absolutely certain: the business of hospitality is centered on one's passions for pleasing people. Passion is the fuel for tenacity, perseverance, and attention to detail that results in this end. It energizes the body and mind to overcome fatigue, fear, and failure. It is the fuel that allows individuals to cope with compelling conditions. One common weakness I find in management (and educators) is overlooking the power of this awesome emotion in their search for prospective leaders and teachers. One can argue that passion alone is not enough, but to lack passion is to lack a vital ingredient for obtaining compliance and team building and, thus, success.

Don't ever be dissuaded from being passionate about your work. Those of you who measure work not in terms of hours but in achievement and pleasure, the ones working sixty to eighty hours a week because you love it, you are marching to the beat of a different drummer in today's society. You really have what it takes to make a difference in the world in which you live. Most of all you have what it takes to make a difference in the lives of the people that you touch. You will often find this place in which you exist lonely. Don't be deterred by the frequent urges of your peers to "Get a life" or "Take it easy or you're going to kill yourself." Life's great fulfillment exists in the pursuit of achieving . . . and that endless pursuit is fueled by passion.

The Power of Passion

It is no accident that all the business books I've ever read include passion as one of the critical factors shaping individual success in the workplace. Passion is a basic requisite for aspiring entrepreneurs: it will allow them to overcome the hardships, failures, challenges, doubts, and uncertainties that come with the territory. Passion is the force that drives people to do their best, to make a difference.

I'm not talking about your run-of-the-mill, everyday kind of desires that all people have; those yearnings don't rise to the level of the driving force that shapes the way people live their lives. I'm talking about PASSION. I'm talking about the "give me liberty or give me death" kind of passion, the "I've got a dream" kind of passion, the "I love you, Juliet" kind of passion. I'm talking about the difference between liking something and loving something, about people who don't just do what they like but love what they do, about not going through the motions but going through *with* emotions. I'm talking about people like Albert Schweitzer, Mother Theresa, Mahatma Gandhi—people with a long-term passion for what they are doing. These are the kind of people Ferdinand Foch was referring to when he said, "The most powerful weapon on earth is the human soul on fire."

Are you passionate about your work? Here's one way to find out: Pretend that you just won $50 million in the lottery and find yourself financially secure for the rest of your life. Now that you have financial independence and don't ever have to earn an income to live comfortably, what would you want to do with the rest of your life?

Whatever you choose to do is probably something you are passionate about doing. Confucius once said, "Choose a job you love, and you will never have to work a day in your life." That's the way entrepreneurs have to feel about what they are doing: they have to have a love for their labor, a passion for what they are trying to achieve. Passion is the fuel that keeps entrepreneurs moving ahead. It gives them the strength to push forward when others say they will be left behind, to persevere when the flashing light says "Abandon ship!" Passion is the ingredient that, when mixed with committed human effort, gives the entrepreneur the opportunity to demonstrate that "impossible" is "possible" waiting to be discovered. Without that passion, an entrepreneur is going to end up an exitpreneur.

One reason I became an entrepreneur was that I realized a lot of people I worked with weren't particularly happy with their jobs and yet they didn't do anything about it. I thought that was hypocritical and I was determined not to turn out like them. They would complain every day that their sales commissions were being cut, or the people they were dealing with or working for weren't ethical. They just felt victimized all the time. I said to myself, "I'm going to take the risk and go out on my own."

Always remember: passion is critical to success. I believe if you love what you're doing, you're going to do it well. And, come to think of it, if you don't enjoy what you're doing, what good is it if you do well, anyway? We spend, on average, forty-five years of our adult lives in the workplace. Life's simply too short to feel bad about your job.

Build It and They Will Come

When you are passionate about a project, anything is possible.

As an example: for years, I wanted to create a themed restaurant based on the tropical rainforest. It started back when I was a teenager. I loved parrots and fish, and I wanted to have a restaurant where they could be displayed for interactive, educational purposes. I also wanted to create an environmental awareness of these beautiful creatures and educate people about what they could do to save the rainforest. The problem was getting investors interested in my idea. Just talking about the project was getting me nowhere. I had to do something far more dramatic and impactful if I ever wanted a shot at financial backing for my idea.

My attention-grabbing idea? I turned my suburban home into a tropical rainforest. I created a jungle home smack dab in the middle of my residential neighborhood. Over a period of a few years, my standard split-level home was transformed into a jungle dwelling complete with rock outcroppings, waterfalls, rivers, layers of fog, mist that rose from the ground, a thatched hut covered with vines on the roof, tiki torches, a twelve-foot neon "paradise" sign, and a full-size replica of an elephant near the front door.

It wasn't easy to create this life-size prototype. I had to knock out rooms to create a greenhouse and I purchased 3,700 bright orange extension cords to hook up to the twenty different sound systems, lights, and fog pumps that provided the jungle noise and mist that floated through the house. Then I had to learn to live with forty tropical birds, two 150-pound tortoises, a baboon, an iguana, and a bevy of tropical fish housed in ten 300-gallon tanks. There were also fifty different animatronic creatures in the house—a collection of mechanized alligators, gorillas, and monkeys. At least I didn't have to feed or clean up after them, but changing their batteries was a real chore. I finally devised a way to get them to run on electricity.

In the bedroom, my bed was constructed to look like it was suspended in a tree. It had waterfalls behind it and mist was rising up in different places throughout the room. Birds and animals moved freely through the area during showings of the house. There were tortoises in the kitchen, parrots in the bathroom, fish everywhere. The humidity from the pumped-in fog and mist destroyed my wallpaper, but I didn't care. Every room, every closet, every hallway of my house was a "scene": an attempt to present my idea of what a rainforest restaurant would look like in actual operation. My house became one huge theatrical set, a life-size stage to visually present my entrepreneurial vision. Overall, it took me three years and almost $400,000 to get the house developed to the point where I felt comfortable showing it to potential investors.

Several of my neighbors weren't exactly thrilled to be living near a jungle habitat. They started a watch group. They even bought walkie-talkies and would update one another on what was happening. When, one day, I heard the front entry chime, I opened the door to what looked like a full-scale crime scene. There were cop cars and officers all over the place. One guy put me up against the door and said he was with the Drug Enforcement Administration and they were going to search the premises for drugs. Because of my huge residential electric bill, they assumed I was growing marijuana in the house. They were astonished when they discovered the tropical rain forest.

Let me tell you: it's not easy to live in a house filled with jungle creatures and surrounded by angry neighbors, all on the off chance that it might help get funding to realize an entrepreneurial dream. What got me through was passion, pure and simple. I knew no venture capitalists were going to invest their money in my far-out concept without actually seeing it, so I transformed my house into my vision of what a rainforest restaurant would look like in order to make them believe in my dream.

It's a Jungle in There

My plan succeeded. It turned out that a fellow Minnesotan, gaming executive and venture capitalist Lyle Berman, bought into the concept and raised the funds necessary to get Rainforest Cafe up and running.

I remember the first time Lyle visited my home. It was early morning and he stopped by on his way to work. I came out to greet him wearing jeans and a khaki shirt, like a safari guide, with a parrot on my shoulder. I led him inside, where he was greeted by forty tropical birds in cages and a baby baboon named Charlie wearing a dress. Jungle foliage, including all kinds of plants and vines, was hanging everywhere. There was a thirty-five-foot waterfall, too, which emptied into a river that snaked though the house and out into the yard. It was filled with pink antifreeze so it wouldn't stop flowing in the winter. To top it off,

I created a mock-up of a retail store with various kinds of rain forest merchandise that looked like a Florida souvenir shop on steroids.

After giving Lyle a tour of the house, I asked him what he thought of it. He told me I needed a psychiatric examination and there was no way he'd invest in my idea. He then asked if he could bring his kids by to see the house, to which I of course agreed. On his next visit, after I gave his kids the grand tour, I again asked Lyle what he thought of my idea.

"Well, your dedication and passion are off the chart," he admitted, "but I'm not buying into this," he claimed. Then he asked if he could bring his parents over.

By the time Lyle's parents had completed the tour, Lyle and I had developed a little ritual. Once the visit was over I'd ask him what he thought. Then I'd anxiously await his answer. This time I reminded Lyle how committed I was to the project, and his response was: "I think you should *be* committed!"

As time passed, Lyle found additional reasons to visit my house. I guess my tenacity and passion for the Rainforest Cafe idea kept growing on him. He kept visiting my house, bringing over other investors for their reactions. Finally, after about two years, Lyle decided to back my idea, and the rest is history: the Rainforest Cafe chain became one of the most successful themed restaurant concepts ever created, and continues that way today under Landry's Restaurants and Tilman Fertitta's leadership.

These days, of course, I create my restaurant concepts in warehouses far from residential neighborhoods, but back then there were no warehouses. I sunk every dollar I had into making my house a themed rainforest restaurant, because I was passionate about the concept and I wanted to see it become a reality.

Passion Trumps Problems

There were times when I truly wondered if my rainforest dream would ever become a reality. After Lyle visited the house more than twenty times in two years without committing himself, you can be damn sure I was frustrated. That's when I decided to make up a sign saying "Lyle Berman made me do this!" and told him if he didn't buy into my restaurant concept, I was going to hang the sign around my neck and jump off the Hennepin Avenue Bridge. (No, I don't think I would have jumped . . . but I would have invited Lyle over for another visit.) That's where passion kicked in. When you're passionate about what you're doing, you'll do whatever needs to be done to reach your objective, to attain your goal. Failure isn't an option; the word *no* isn't in your vocabulary.

Being passionate doesn't totally shield you from moments of doubt, unfortunately. There were nights I'd go to bed and have trouble sleeping. I remember looking in the mirror and wondering if I really was crazy. I told myself I was neurotic. It was an emotional time for me. I didn't know how long I could keep things going; I just knew the Rainforest Cafe was a great idea, and I couldn't let it go. I wanted to share my passion for the tropical rainforest with everyone. I discovered quickly that everything I developed creatively would be based on the five senses of touch, taste, smell, sound, and sight.

Of course, the DEA raid didn't help matters, but it wasn't my biggest headache. (In fact, when the agents found out what was really in the house, several of them brought their kids over to visit the place and some even purchased stock in the company.) No, the worst moment for me involved a disagreement with the gas company. It was over bills. I hadn't been paying them and, even more troublesome, I connected up the gas meter a few times after the company had turned it off for nonpayment.

Things came to a head one Friday night when a convoy of trucks showed up in the cul-de-sac where my house was located. It was the gas company. I guess management was tired of me finding ways to turn the gas back on. The workers dug a twenty-five-foot-deep hole in the road and shut off the main gas valve to my house. Then they covered up the hole and prepared the road to be repaved.

I was desperate! It was the beginning of winter and the gas supplied heat to the house. Without it, my animals would die. Luckily, it wasn't too cold yet and I was able to get by with electric heaters. I called the gas company and begged its representatives to turn the gas back on. It took me three days to raise the money to get the workers to come back. I ended up having to pay the bill plus the cost of digging and repaving the road. The neighbors were none too happy, either. Believe me, that was one time that even *my* passion flagged a bit. But, in the final analysis, I picked myself up and moved on, reminding myself of the words penned by Arthur Buddhold: "Follow your passion, and success will follow you." That's how the Rainforest Cafe was born.

And that's why I make no apologies for living passionately, and neither should you.

CHAPTER 3

Ambition: Taking Your Passions Public

"Ambition is the germ from which all growth of nobleness proceeds."

—THOMAS DUNN

Self-examination Question:
Do you desire and/or seek public recognition for what you have accomplished?

There are individuals who think ambition is a bad thing. Perhaps that's why, for some people, the term has a negative connotation, conjuring up images of backstabbing corporate climbers. I'm not one of these individuals. I believe that ambition, like passion, drives people to realize their full potential: to become all they are capable of becoming in both their personal and business lives.

I didn't come from a rich home. In fact, we had to scrimp and save just to make ends meet. Yet I was able to realize my dream of becoming a successful entrepreneur because I was ambitious; I was driven to succeed. When I was young, I would get up earlier than all my friends and go to work. By the time they awoke, around eleven o'clock in the morning, I had already been working for four hours and had $20 stashed in my pocket. Today, I continue to get up and work hours before my other team members show up at the office. It's those hours before nine o'clock in the morning that have made the crucial difference in my success.

Of course, being born wealthy hardly hurts a person's chances of succeeding in today's competitive world, but it is neither necessary nor sufficient to guarantee success. If you are short on cash but long on ambition, limited in funds but unlimited in your commitment to get ahead and make a name for yourself, you can achieve greatness. Desire beats dollars every day of the week. I'd rather bet on a person with ambition than on a guy with money who thinks the world owes him a living. I'll take commitment over cash every time when it comes to predicting entrepreneurial success. For those with ambition, the good news is the "American Dream" is alive and well: you needn't be born with a silver spoon in your mouth to achieve a generous portion of success in your life.

In my opinion, being hungry, feeling economically pinched, can actually stimulate the creative juices and fire up a person to achieve more than someone who is financially comfortable and just doesn't have the same level of need to produce something of significance. Maybe that's why I resonate with the concept of the "starving artist." In fact, maybe that's what the term is all about: being without, being willing to forego normal creature comforts in search of perfection in one's work.

Passion + Ambition Yields Success (It P.A.Y.S.)!

In my seminars and discussions with other businesspeople, I'm often surprised that people either don't see the importance of ambition for entrepreneurial success, or they treat "passion" and "ambition" as the same thing. In fact, passion and ambition have a symbiotic relationship when it comes to entrepreneurs. Think of passion and ambition as the peanut butter and jelly of entrepreneurial success: They work together to create a better outcome. Passion provides the fuel that drives a person to create a service or product and ambition supplies the desire to get that service or product out to the public. Without ambition, a passionate person might create great things but not have the urge to share them.

I knew a writer who was that way. He loved to write and had a passion for his craft. He would sit day after day at his computer creating works of fiction, but he'd never try and get them published. When I asked him about his reluctance to share his books with others, he said the satisfaction of writing was reward enough for him. But was that it? Who knows? Perhaps he was afraid of rejection or public reaction to his work. Whatever the reason, here was a man with a passion who lacked the ambition to bring his creations into the world. He was like the proverbial tree that fell in the forest and no one was there to hear it.

Most people aren't like my friend, the writer. If they produce something they believe has value, they'll try to market it. What varies mightily is the degree of effort they will expend to get the most from their discovery or product. Ambitious people will push what they have to the limit while people of less ambition might have something of equal value, but their lack of drive will affect its marketplace impact.

Passion by itself isn't enough. Producing the greatest invention or work of art on Earth isn't enough. It doesn't become significant until the person of passion who created it has enough ambition to share it with others. That is the critical link between passion and ambition and why both must be present in people who want to reach their full potential as entrepreneurs.

Many years ago I came across something called "The Artist's Credo," by Douglas Bloch, who wrote *Listening to Your Inner Voice*. It represents how I feel about art and the artistic product. One portion of that credo is germane to the relationship between passion and ambition (see pg 229 for the credo in full):

> *After the creation is born, it needs to be shared*
> *with others. No one creates in a vacuum.*
> *It is only when the vision is successfully*
> *communicated to its intended audience that it*
> *truly comes alive.*

Sadly, in most cases, passion without ambition is passion wasted. Successful entrepreneurship requires both the creation of a valued product or service and its introduction into the marketplace. Entrepreneurs with no ambition to share the fruits of their passion will never be as successful as entrepreneurs with passion and the ambition to bring their creations to the attention of the consuming public.

Ambition helps passion succeed. As J. C. Penney once said, "Give me a stock clerk with a goal and I'll give you a man who will make history. Give me a man with no goals and I'll give you a stock clerk."

CHAPTER 4

I Dream . . . Therefore I Can

"Happy are those who dream dreams and are ready to pay the price to make them come true."
—Leon Joseph Cardinal Suenens

Self-examination Question:
Do you enjoy using your imagination to dream up new ideas, products, or services that could generate profits in the marketplace?

An important talent entrepreneurs need to possess is the ability to dream—to see things that others have not yet envisioned. It provides the means to imagine and create new products and/or services that nobody else has thought of or, at least, not exploited appropriately. Passion often serves as the springboard for these dreams. When you allow yourself to feel truly passionate about something, it spawns ideas, and those lead to other ideas and then, if you're me, you have a room full of dinosaurs in your office and a booming business behind them.

Of course, not all dreams are created equal. When I'm speaking of "dreams" in the context of entrepreneurial success, I'm not referring to the kind of dreams people have while sleeping (although some ideas have come during such moments) or to "daydreams," where individuals are simply entertaining themselves with fantasies that have no economic implications. In the vast majority of cases, the dreams that bring business success are those experienced by entrepreneurs as they allow their imaginations free rein in experiencing what goes on around them in their everyday lives while thinking about what services or products they might create to change life in a manner that would bring them financial gain.

An interesting example of how the dream process works to spur entrepreneurial endeavors and success is provided in the movie *Bugsy*, where the main character (played by Warren Beatty) is driving across the Mojave Desert and suddenly stops his car to get out. He peers into the desert wasteland, considers the desolation all around him, and envisions a gambling casino that will eventually turn Las Vegas into the gaming capital of the world.

I experienced a parallel example of this creative vision while crossing the South Dakota Badlands on my motorcycle. I, too, stopped along the side of the deserted road, and, as I stared into the desolate terrain, I saw a place where dinosaurs once roamed. I pictured a restaurant based on the giant beasts. That image eventually morphed into the highly successful chain of T-Rex restaurants now operating throughout the United States.

Entrepreneurs must be willing to dream. They must be constantly looking for that new idea, new service, new product, new angle. They must realize that conceiving of an idea is not only the necessary first step to entrepreneurial success—it is often the most important step in the journey. Don't be afraid to give your mind free rein. As Tom Robbins wisely observes, "To achieve the impossible, it is precisely the unthinkable that must be thought." If you knew you could not fail, what would you attempt to do?

Don't be afraid to dream, and dream big. Anyone can puncture people's dreams and tell them they're unrealistic, but it takes an unusual person to know the value of planning big, shooting high, and keeping the upward look.

Successful entrepreneurs tend to be optimists; they have the kind of "positive thinking" attitude that allows them to dream and not get bogged down by naysayers and doubters who would challenge their inspirations. Entrepreneurs are, in many ways, futurists. That is, they love to live in the future, dream about the future, talk about the future—and they are always urging people around them to do the same.

One might wonder if there is ever a time that an aspiring entrepreneur should think "small" when looking for a successful venture. I believe the personal character and creative process of individual entrepreneurs will play a role in determining if they want to aim for a piece of the Earth or shoot for the stars. It's in my nature to "think big." Why would you want to make $850,000 a year owning a pizzeria, when you could use the same amount of hard work and passion to earn much more? I'd rather focus my thoughts on places that do a minimum of $15 million yearly.

Dreaming big also gives a person a better chance at succeeding big. When Michael Phelps won a record-shattering eight gold medals in the Beijing Olympics he said, "I saw quotes that [Mark] Spitz's seven medals record would be impossible to duplicate, that it would never happen. But if you dream as big as you can dream, anything is possible."

As a "dream driven" entrepreneur, and in a capitalist system where dreams can still come true, one should never underestimate their importance in achieving success in life. Use your mind to incubate, nourish, and bring your dreams to fruition. Remember, the Lord gave us two ends, one to sit on and one to think with. Success depends on which one you use: heads you win, tails you lose!

One of the most inspiring articles I ever read was published in *Fortune* magazine back in 1996. It describes how some of America's greatest entrepreneurs—people like Henry Ford, Walt Disney, C. E. Woolman (Delta Airlines), and Steve Jobs—took their dreams to dynasties by developing their ideas in the obscurity of their garages (referred to by *Fortune* as "America's secret weapon" in the battle for economic supremacy).

Always remember that some of the most memorable and successful entrepreneurial undertakings started with a dream. Keep dreams foremost in your entrepreneurial arsenal and you will always have creative firepower at your disposal. I think this poem by Langston Hughes says it all:

> *Hold fast to dreams*
> *For if dreams die*
> *Life is a broken-winged bird*
> *That cannot fly.*
> *Hold fast to dreams*
> *For when dreams go*
> *Life is a barren field*
> *Frozen with snow.*

CHAPTER 5

The Multitasker

"A person who learns to juggle six balls will be more skilled than the person who never tries to juggle more than three."

—MARILYN VOS SAVANT

Self-examination Question:
Can you comfortably and successfully perform two or more tasks at the same time?

S everal years ago a client walked into my office for the first time and saw me sitting at my desk. "You looked like the mission control guy they cut to on CNN when the Space Shuttle crew says something important, like 'Houston, I think we have a problem,'" he told me later. "You were speaking into a cell phone in one hand while checking your BlackBerry in the other. I looked at your desk and saw three different computer screens, each run by a separate computer. There were also three separate landline phones within reach." (In fact, the client had failed to notice a laptop computer laying on the floor, a television, two fax machines, and—to complete the communication cornucopia—a designated "red phone" with a direct international line to my home in Acapulco, Mexico.)

All that communication equipment is on my desk for a purpose. I use it! It's not unusual for me to carry on two, three, or even four conversations at the same time while tracking the computer screens on my desk. It's called "multitasking," and it's a skill I believe all entrepreneurs will need to have if they want to stay competitive in the new realities of computer- and smartphone-driven business in the twenty-first century.

When it comes to multitasking, I guess I'm one of the lucky ones. I seem to have the personality for it. Ever since I was a kid, people would comment about me doing multiple things at once—for example, my restless need to keep "several balls in the air" or my short attention span. As I grew older, psychologists began giving my behavior a name: Attention Deficit Disorder (ADD). They were usually referring to my habit of doing several things at once, often in a hyper (or, as I like to think of it, highly energetic) fashion. I find this kind of behavior—what I call "hyper-tasking"—to be quite satisfying, yet some of my friends and business associates think I should avoid doing it. One of my partners once warned me, "If you take your eyes off the ball and people think the creator of Rainforest Cafe is developing other concepts, they're going to think you're a flake. Our stock prices are going to go down, so let's just make this one work. They will think you lost your passion or direction."

My partner could not envision a person driven passionately about more than one project at a time. The fact was that I did keep my eye on the ball; it's just that, like a juggler, I happened to have several balls in the air at the time. In fact, I firmly believe that one of the most important talents (or skills) an entrepreneur can have is the ability to multitask. Entrepreneurs often have three or four or five things going on simultaneously. It's a disservice to tell them that they should be focused, because they *are* focused but are thinking on multiple levels. They can track six balls at once. It's a gift, and they should embrace it.

Thinking on multiple levels works for me because it stimulates my creative juices. If I want to think about custom motorcycles one day and French saxophone players the next, let me do that. If I'm at the rock, mineral, and fossil show in Arizona researching for T-Rex, why can't I find something that would work in my Asian restaurant concept? If I see butterflies at the state fair and the sight gives me an idea for a chandelier, why can't I do that? That's my prerogative.

But here is the true value of multitasking: it allows you to have several concepts or ideas going at once. That means that, when investors come knocking, you don't have just one shot to get their business, you have several opportunities. It's like a car dealership: there's more than one model to choose from, which gives customers more choices—and thus a greater chance they'll find something that suits them.

On several occasions, my ability to multitask is what has been directly responsible for landing major deals. For instance, when Disney became interested in our T-Rex restaurant, the investors also liked our Asian concept, Yak & Yeti. They told me they would only do T-Rex if they could have the Asian restaurant, too. Well, I certainly didn't complain about that requirement. If I hadn't been working on two concepts at once, that deal would have never happened. Other times, I've walked investors through my warehouses and they've passed by three concepts with no interest and then bought into the fourth.

The point is that my multitasking behavior allows me to give investors greater choice when it comes to investing in our projects. This kind of thinking offers more choices to business partners.

Whether you're just starting your entrepreneurial career or you're a seasoned veteran, when people tell you to focus on one thing at a time and stop multitasking, don't listen! You have a special talent, and you should be grateful you do. The future belongs to us multitaskers, so get on with all those things you were doing with a smile on your face.

CHAPTER 6

You've Learned Your ABCs, Now Practice Your CBAs

"Sometimes the best way to move forward is to move backward."

—Anonymous

Self-examination Question:
Do you have the desire to create something new, the strength of conviction to believe your creation will be successful, and the reservoir of energy necessary to thrust it into the marketplace?

I n school you learn your ABCs. Well, if you want to become an entrepreneur you've got to practice your CBAs. The entrepreneurial process is a matter of **C**onceiving, **B**elieving, and **A**chieving.

Conceive: Come Up with a Product or Service That People Will Buy

An entrepreneur without something to sell is like a consumer with no money to buy. It's a losing proposition. Without the ability to create a marketable service or product, any would-be entrepreneur is doomed to failure. Even the most well-intentioned, passionate, ambitious individuals can't make the sale if they have nothing to offer. This is where dreaming comes in. Whether you are an aspiring or an established entrepreneur, you should always be dreaming of new ways to make your mark in the world. And don't be afraid to dream big. As children we dreamed big, but somewhere along the way to adulthood, most of us forgot how to do it. We need to recapture this childhood ability to fantasize and dream large.

Don't be afraid to release the inner child in you and give it free rein when thinking about entrepreneurial ideas. It is remarkable how our educational system and those around us tend to quash this "childlike" quality of imagination that can be such a fertile ground for creating new products and services. Think, imagine, allow your mind to roam free, and revel in that childlike world where boundaries are limitless and anything is possible. Don't worry about constraints: *conceive*. They'll be plenty of time to refine your ideas once you come up with them.

If You Believe, You Can Succeed

Many potentially successful entrepreneurs fail because they lack the necessary belief in themselves to push forward with their products or discoveries. As we have seen earlier, all the passion in the world is wasted if a person lacks the ambition to bring his creation out into the open.

Many decades ago, a famous clergyman and author, Norman Vincent Peale, wrote an optimistic book extolling the virtues of a positive mindset, appropriately titled *The Power of Positive Thinking*. When all is said and done, the book's main thesis can be boiled down to one basic principle, both simple and profound: If you believe, you can succeed.

It is critical for entrepreneurs to believe in themselves and what they are doing. As we saw in Chapter 1, this is because the very nature of the entrepreneurial life comes with risk, failure, and a hearty portion of skeptics ready to dismiss your ideas. Because the essence of entrepreneurism is innovation and change, the entrepreneur must often challenge or change the status quo. Most people are not comfortable with this action, which is why there aren't many entrepreneurs, particularly when compared to the number of individuals who choose to work for a predictable paycheck in jobs that have structured rules and established ways of doing things.

Stability and familiarity are comforting conditions for most people. Entrepreneurs have no such comforts; their challenge is to create new things, often in the face of fierce opposition from those who object to what they are doing. To function in that kind of environment requires a strong sense of self-confidence, a belief in yourself and what you are doing.

"If you believe, you can succeed" are potent words that every entrepreneur should take to heart. It is the proper entrepreneurial

mindset. Should you doubt this truth, consider the observation
made by Henry Ford, one of the world's greatest entrepreneurs:
"If you think that you can, or you think that you can't . . . either
way, you're right."

And if you're still having trouble believing in yourself, take
heart and strength from the words of an anonymous poet who
reminds us, correctly, that "It's All in a State of Mind":

> *If you think you are beaten you are.*
> *If you think you dare not, you won't.*
> *If you like to win but don't think you can,*
> *It's almost a cinch that you won't.*

> *Life's battles don't always go*
> *To the Bigger or stronger man,*
> *But sooner or later the man who wins*
> *Is the fellow who thinks he can.*

> *Think big and your deeds will grow;*
> *Think small and you'll fall behind.*
> *Think that you can and you will . . .*
> *It's all in a state of mind.*

Achieve: Get Out There and Sell What You've Created!

They say that success is 10 percent inspiration and 90 percent
perspiration. In the case of entrepreneurs, the percentages are
probably a bit different: maybe a bit closer to a 50–50 split.
Nevertheless, no entrepreneur can afford to create in a vacuum (as

we have seen in "The Artist's Credo"). Passion without ambition, as earlier emphasized, is passion wasted. Please remember that creating something that will rock the marketplace is only half the battle; getting the marketplace to take note of what you have achieved is the other half. The greatest product or service in the world—like the tree falling in the forest with no one there to hear it—will go unnoticed if the entrepreneur lacks the ambition to get behind it and work to *achieve* the fruits of what you have created.

Be enthusiastic about what you have conceived. Such enthusiasm will positively impact how you believe and what you can achieve. Ralph Waldo Emerson said:

> *Enthusiasm is one of the most powerful*
> *engines of success. When you do a thing, do*
> *it with all your might. Put your whole soul*
> *into it. Stamp it with your own personality.*
> *Be active, be energetic, be enthusiastic and*
> *faithful, and you will accomplish your*
> *objective. Nothing great was ever achieved*
> *without enthusiasm.*

Great words to live by . . . and profit from.

🌿

Conceive. Believe. Achieve. These are the main ingredients in the recipe for entrepreneurial success. Throw in a pinch of passion, a dash of dreaming, and some essence of ambition and, voila, you've got what you need to get things cooking. Now let's take some time to focus on the product you're getting ready to serve.

SECTION II

PRODUCT

CHAPTER 7

Be Excellent or Be Gone

"There are no shortcuts to any place worth going."
—Anonymous

Self-examination Question:
Are you willing to take the extra time
and effort necessary to create a product
or service that is excellent rather
than acceptable?

Because creating themed restaurants is what I do for a living, I tend to be a self-appointed critic when visiting other eating establishments. Whether it involves the quality of the food or the overall ambiance of the place, I'm always on the lookout for ways to enhance the dining experience. This can sometimes create unintended consequences, a few quite memorable in scope.

Several years ago, I was visiting Japan and stopped at a famous Tokyo restaurant for some food. In my never-ending quest for gustatory excellence, I challenged a veteran sushi chef on the freshness of his product. (The fact that it was my first visit to Japan and the chef was only inches away from my body with an extremely large, sharp knife in his hand didn't detour me from my culinary criticism. I was convinced the sushi simply wasn't up to par.) Though the chef defended his product that day, I heard after the fact from a Japanese friend that the chef later admitted to a colleague that the sushi was, in fact, a day old.

I suspect the average customer at that Tokyo restaurant wouldn't have noticed the sushi's lack of freshness, but that's not the point. It's all about excellence and giving your best, even if you might get away with doing less. Is getting away with less really worth it? Your work is a reflection of yourself, so why would you want a mirror of mediocrity?

Ever since my earliest days as an entrepreneur, I've been guided by two quotes that I had framed and placed on the wall over my desk:

"When you're out of quality, you're out of business."

"The noblest search is the search for excellence."

Aspiring and practicing entrepreneurs take note: if you keep these two thoughts in your mind, and use them as guiding principles in your entrepreneurial journey, your chances of reaching a successful destination will be greatly enhanced.

I have no way of knowing what product or service you are developing or what you plan to sell or provide. The purpose of this book is not to give you suggestions in these areas. Rather, it is to remind you of the importance of establishing a baseline of excellence in whatever you create and, also, to suggest some ways that excellence can be achieved and maintained. Your reputation will be riding on the quality of your work. It's worth the extra effort to make sure your reputation is excellent.

CHAPTER 8

Sweat the Small Stuff: The Importance of Paying Attention to Detail

Self-examination Question:
Do you believe that it's often the little things that make a big difference between success and failure in business?

There's an old saying that "the devil's in the details." To my mind, that's where excellence resides, too.

Conrad Hilton, famous for the chain of high-end hotels that bear his name, was a man who knew this concept well. To make sure the quality of his establishments remained high, Conrad would make regular, announced visits to his properties to check things out. The story is that if, upon arriving at one of his hotels, he noted there was a lightbulb burned out in the lobby, he'd book himself a room for an extra day or two. The reason? If, knowing that the big boss was coming, the staff had still failed to replace burned-out lightbulbs properly, Hilton wondered what else might be amiss at the hotel. The burned-out bulb was the canary in the coal mine suggesting that service standards might be lagging. Maybe there were no problems and the lightbulb problem was a false alarm, but it was worth an extra day or two of a busy corporate executive's time to verify that things were right and service was up to Hilton standards.

Hilton understood that small things are what determine that level of excellence: add them up and it's the small things that determine the overall quality of an organization. Therefore, attention to detail, sweating the small stuff, was absolutely essential to obtaining and maintaining great customer service, the metric by which this hotel executive measured organizational excellence.

People often fail to realize just how important attention to detail is, both in business and in one's personal life. People who don't sweat the small stuff can lose some big stuff (as in big bucks), as was the case with the man who made a minor typing error in selling a bottle of Allsopp's Arctic Ale on eBay. The problem was he spelled it *Allsops*—a mistake that resulted in only two bids and a sale price of $304. When the winning bidder turned around and relisted the bottle on eBay, this time with the correct spelling, the listing generated 157 bidders and a sale price of $503,300! A half-million-dollar difference—that's gotta sting. (It's not confirmed that the bidder actually paid the $503,300, but wine experts believe the rare bottle of ale is worth at least five figures.)

One of the reasons I have had a successful relationship building themed restaurants for Disney is because the company liked our extreme attention to detail. I consider this the ultimate compliment, because Disney's excellence is built on attention to detail. Go to any Disney theme park and watch the staff (particularly the executives) as they walk through the property. If they see a piece of paper on the ground, they'll stop and pick it up. They sweat the small stuff.

That's how they got to be big stuff.

In developing projects, I'm always reminding my team to focus on details, to get things right in all aspects of our operations. It is advice I give . . . and follow *rigorously.* Sometimes I'll miss a detail and I'm always thankful when someone brings the oversight to my attention.

I remember one example in particular. It involved our Winter Wonderland restaurant concept, specifically the model railroad trains that run on elevated tracks around the display we constructed. One business associate, when touring our facility, noted that the locomotive pulling the string of freight cars had no smoke coming out of its stack. I looked closer, and, sure enough, there was a smokestack and no smoke.

I don't know how I missed it! I even remember as a kid having to put capsules in the engine of my own model train to create the smoke. Once the mistake was pointed out to me, I saw that the effect simply wasn't the same without the smoke. Maybe it seems like a small thing to you, but, to me, my omission was a step backward from excellence; it compromised the quality of what we were trying to create. It was a problem that needed fixing.

It's not easy to stay focused on the small stuff, particularly since many entrepreneurs see themselves as "big-picture thinkers" (and, in fact, I'm sure they are and probably need to be if they aren't). But the truly successful entrepreneur has to have what has been called the "helicopter view": the ability to gain enough mental altitude to see the big picture while retaining the ability to descend, hover, and see the details, too. You need to think big, but also focus small.

A few days ago, I was bringing a client into the office for a tour. I noticed a cigarette butt on the walkway right in front of our door. I don't know how long it had been there, but I stopped, bent down, and picked it up. The client was amazed. In his eyes, he saw the president of a company doing a menial task, something most executives would ignore or leave for others to do. "I'm not sure I would have even spotted that cigarette butt, let alone picked it up," he said. He then added, "If you take that much pride in the appearance of your property and have the eye to spot small imperfections it probably reflects on the quality of what I'm about to see."

Little things.

Sweating the small stuff.

People notice. They see you care passionately and appreciate your attention to detail. It helps turn them into loyal clients, customers, and investors.

Noticing the small stuff can also enhance the marketing and

presentation of your product. I think back to early architectural renderings of the design for the interior of my Backfire BBQ restaurant. We'd had a really smart team working on the concept, but when I got the designs, they just looked wrong. It took me a few minutes to figure it out: the architects had forgotten to add any people, so the restaurant looked totally dead. The bar was simply deserted. We wanted, of course, to portray a bustling restaurant full of people, food, and energy—a venue that looked like the place to be, not someplace that was just hit by the plague.

When I pointed out this problem to my architects, one of the partners told me, "You know, in twenty-five years, nobody has ever pointed out what you just spotted. It really makes sense." I just shook my head.

Attention to detail: it makes a difference.

Excellent service because of attention to detail is what can transform a passerby into a loyal customer. And when investors notice, it's all the better.

Sweat the small stuff. It'll help you earn the big stuff!

CHAPTER 9

Always Be on the Lookout for Your Next Big Thing

Self-examination Question:
As you observe your world around you do you make a consistent, conscious effort to ask yourself: "Is there something here I could change (by providing a service or product) that would bring me financial gain?"

One thing I learned as a young man has helped me to this day: always be on the lookout for products or services that people need, and then be prepared to provide those needs in exchange for adequate compensation.

This is the prime directive for any aspiring entrepreneur to follow, as it is the very essence of what entrepreneurship is all about. The sooner you train yourself to look around for opportunities to provide desired goods and services for profit, the sooner you will achieve entrepreneurial success.

Opportunity is waiting for you to find it! It is amazing to discover just how many of these opportunities actually exist once you get in the habit of looking for them. It's just a matter of training yourself to automatically scan your environment for what I call "enhancement gaps"—the difference between what you are seeing and what you could create to make what you are seeing better by providing some product or service.

My first chance to make use of this principle occurred when I was just thirteen years old. During summers, I worked as one of several cabana boys at the Silver Gull Beach Club in Breezy Point, New York. My official duty was to get the cabanas ready for use each day by putting the chairs and umbrellas out, and then clearing everything away each evening. It was simple and straightforward, but certainly less than demanding.

However, during my first week on the job, I noticed there was a group of adult men who played cards around some makeshift tables near the swimming pool. Sometimes, one of the men would call me over to run an errand for him, such as getting him a sandwich or some extra ice for his drink. For this service, I would get a tip, sometimes as much as $10. So I started hanging around the card players more often and, sure enough, once the guys saw me there on a consistent basis, they started asking me to run more errands and do them more favors. Hot towels, cold towels, pastrami sandwiches, umbrellas, sunglasses, it didn't matter: I never failed to honor a request.

I was making a hell of a lot more money being their gofer than I was as a cabana boy, as I'd generally score a $5 tip for my efforts. If any of "my" card players wanted something, I made sure they got it. I became known as the go-to guy for anything. One time, a player got a flat tire in the parking lot. He told me to take care of it and I had it repaired within an hour. I never said no to any request. *No* is a word I hate; it isn't in my vocabulary. I had become a card-table concierge and was being paid handsomely for my services.

The longer I watched the game, the more I realized there was a treasure trove of additional money that could be made. For example, I noted that some guys would fight for certain seats at the table (usually their "lucky" chair or a spot in the sun), so I started reserving their favorite chairs for them. Of course, the players showed their gratitude by giving me generous tips. I used my tip money to upgrade the playing environment. I purchased new tables and chairs and charged a "rental" fee to play. The men paid me a $5 sit-down fee. What had started as a one-table game expanded, under my direction, to a three-table game. I was actually running a card room and all the players were happy because I was giving them what they wanted: a better playing environment and someone to run errands for them when they didn't want to get things for themselves. I was turning a tidy profit and providing a needed service at the same time.

There was more. I noticed that the guys could use up to seven packs of cards a day during their play. With three tables, that meant twenty-one packs of cards were needed to keep the action going. I decided I could make extra money if I supplied the cards directly to the players, rather than having them purchase the decks for retail at the local drugstore. I found out the brand of the cards and located the manufacturer's distribution point, which turned out to be in Far Rockaway, three bus rides away from the club. Every week, I would make the trip to the distribution point and buy several cases of brand-new cards. Because I bought in bulk, at wholesale prices, I was able to mark up the decks 150 percent and still charge the players less for the cards than they would have paid at the local drugstore. Plus, I saved them the trip to the store in the process.

Although the games were only played on Saturdays and Sundays, I found myself making about $700 a weekend based on my card sales, table rentals, and tips garnered from running errands for the players. Meanwhile, amazingly, none of the other cabana boys had any idea about the kind of money I was raking in.

The following summer, I added additional money-making wrinkles to my card-table operation. I purchased a refrigerator, stuck it out near the tables with an extension cord, and stocked it with iced tea, lemonade, and orange juice—I even tried to slip in some vodka (without success, as I was still only fourteen). I started selling the drinks directly to the players, keeping both the markup on the beverages and the tips I got for bringing them to the tables. I got to know each player's favorite drink and made sure I had enough stock never to run out. Every time I brought a drink to the table, it was another $5 in my pocket, plus the profit margin I made between my cost for the refreshments and the markup I charged the player. (Remember, I had no help. This was a one-man show.)

I even concocted an idea for saving money on ice. In the early days of my operation, I used to pay for bags of ice from a nearby convenience store and haul them to the club. Then I realized it would be cheaper (and, by that, I mean *free*) and less hassle to just take ice from the kitchen at night when no one was around and use it to keep the drinks cold. I also started running errands for the families of the players, tapping into yet another income stream. The players started asking me to deliver drinks to their wives, and they'd tip me for doing so. They guys even began betting on how fast I could run an errand. I usually made money on that wager, too. The cash was rolling in at an extraordinary rate.

Sadly, it was around this time that I made my major mistake: I started bragging to my cousin about how much money I was making. He had worked at the club for five years as a cabana boy, and when he heard about my $700-dollar weekends, he bounced off the wall. "Seven hundred dollars for two days work?" he said with disbelief, "You've gotta be kidding me!" He spread the news around, bragging as a very proud relative about my business acumen.

It was a very short time later that the general manager pulled me into his office.

He was nice about it, but he made it clear my gravy days were at an end. "You make more money than I do," he explained. "I've been in business a hell of a long time and you're one hell of an entrepreneur. We love you and would love you to stay on and be part of our team, but we're taking over the card tables."

I, of course, wanted no part of it. I had built the business through my purchasing skills, sweat equity, and great service. Now the club wanted to take over what I had created. When

I didn't accept the club's offer, the manager hired one guy and two girls to do what I had done by myself . . . and my card-table management days were over.

But the lesson I learned would last a lifetime: observing your surroundings to see what you can do to make things better is a surefire formula for turning a profit. This is what entrepreneurism is all about. It's about spotting a need that isn't being fulfilled and providing that fulfillment.

Go forth and spot some enhancement gaps. They're out there, just waiting to be exploited. Your next financially profitable idea, product, or service might be no further away than something you observe the next time you walk out your front door.

CHAPTER 10

Research and Development: Learn It If You Want to Earn It

Self-examination Question:
Even though it can be costly, are you willing to undertake sufficient R&D in exploring new ideas, products, and services?

When we opened our first T-Rex restaurant in Kansas City, I was approached by a reporter who had just finished touring the facility. He had spent the better part of an hour looking at the animatronic dinosaurs, the prehistoric décor, the themed dining rooms with ice caves and meteor showers, the fossil dig, and the retail store. "How long did it take you to come up with all this?" he asked.

"Our team spent five years and $15 million working on the concept before we ever earned a dime," I replied honestly.

The reporter was shocked that it cost so much in money and time to make our dream a reality.

He's not alone. Many people underestimate the amount of research and development (R&D) that goes into bringing a successful concept, product, or service to market. In fact, in my area of specialization, I honestly believe that one of the biggest mistakes restaurant owners make is underestimating how much time and research-and-development money they need to spend to make their concept a reality and take it over the top.

In general, I believe that entrepreneurs pay far too little attention to R&D when taking steps to create a product or service and devising the best strategy for marketing what they intend to offer. I understand their attitude. A lot of individuals and businesses don't like to spend a lot of time and money up front in researching and developing the best way to achieve an excellent result. They want to get to the marketplace quickly, at minimal cost, so they can start showing a return on investment (ROI). Sadly, such an attitude can actually cost more than it saves.

One advantage of R&D is to discover, before too much time and money is wasted, which undertakings are viable and which ones are not. I truly believe that more focused attention on R&D will enhance greatly the chances for succeeding with any viable entrepreneurial undertaking. I am convinced that the extensive R&D Schussler Creative undertook in developing the Rainforest Cafe was a major reason for its success. It was through the painstaking study of the Rainforest concept that I came up with my "11 Commandments" for making a themed restaurant profitable. They constitute the foundation for developing new restaurant projects.

My 11 Commandments for Creating Successful Themed Restaurants

1. **Entertainment:** This is the "hook" we use to get people interested in the environment and education we offer.
2. **Education:** We use education to encourage the general public to learn and care for our planet.
3. **Environment:** We truly care about what is happening to our planet.
4. **Employees:** We are only as good as the people around us and we depend on our employees to help us be the best that we can be.
5. **Earnings:** ROI is what makes our projects viable.
6. **Sight:** Visual stimulation excites the customer about our concept.
7. **Sound:** Audio stimulation helps create a realistic dining experience.
8. **Smell:** We use scent to make the environment more pleasant for the customer.
9. **Touch:** Tactile stimulation is important to the overall experience enjoyed by our customers.

10. **Taste:** If it tastes great on the palate, then it will be great for the profit.

11. **Passion:** This is what drives us to create to the best of our ability.

To increase our business profitability, we are constantly hiring focus groups to test our ideas and get a better idea of how successful our products and services might be in the marketplace. For example, when we were designing our T-Rex restaurant, we brought in groups of youngsters to test the viability of our retail offerings and the "fossil dig" (a special archeological sandpit in one area of the restaurant) where kids could use shovels to unearth dinosaur bones and other prehistoric treasures. Through that experience, we learned exactly where the kids liked to spend the most time, and we were able to plan accordingly.

Because of the amount of time and effort you will need to commit to a project to ensure its quality and success, it's important that you like your idea in the first place. Then you need to submerge yourself in it fully. This often involves spending a lot of time in libraries and on the Internet researching what interests you. In general, the bigger the project, the more time you'll need to spend learning about it.

Part of the thrill I get from being an entrepreneur is the education I receive along the way. Take T-Rex as an example. I didn't know anything about dinosaurs until I spent countless hours researching them. The learning process didn't stop there, either. We're still experimenting with dinosaurs: How long will the skins last? What is the impact of UV rays on the dinosaurs' skin? What kind of upkeep will be required to keep our mechanical models operational? It's really never-ending.

But it's well worth it. Research and development, just like passion, is an engine of success. Without R&D, you can't possibly do your best in creating and marketing your product and service. Research and development is the most direct route to that destination called excellence, the place every entrepreneur should want to call home. It's a route well worth taking.

CHAPTER 11

Make Improvements—Before and After

Self-examination Question:
Once your creation is in the marketplace,
do you still look for ways to improve it?

I have encountered many entrepreneurs who rush their products or services to market too quickly. There are numerous reasons for taking such action, including the need to recoup costs, meet investor or company deadlines, or make a living—or simply the urge to see one's handiwork out there. The problem with moving too quickly, however, is the impact it has on the creative process. Great ideas, like great wines, need proper aging: time to bring out their full flavor and quality. Rushing the creative process can lead to results that are viable but below the standard of excellence that could have been achieved had the entrepreneur taken additional time to let her ideas fully ripen.

The creative process is not cut-and-dried like a scientific equation. No one can give you a mathematical formula that will reveal with certainty exactly when your idea has reached that perfect moment of maturity to harvest. For most innovative people, that point becomes a matter of feel, a sense of when things are ready. However, this feeling is very fragile and can be easily disrupted or distorted by pressure to get to market more quickly.

Most entrepreneurs don't have the luxury of limitless deadlines and unlimited funds. Thus, they must strike a balance between allowing their ideas ample time to mature while still meeting the demands of their backers and making a living. My hope is you'll do your best to give your ideas time to breathe and not push forward so rapidly you short-circuit your creative process.

In my career, I've certainly seen the ways allowing yourself creative breathing space can change a product from acceptable to exceptional.

Several years ago, I set out to create a themed restaurant that served up a barbecue-type menu and featured motorcycles, cars, jukeboxes, and some colorful neon signs. I decided to call the concept "America's Roadhouse." After letting the idea incubate for a while I decided the restaurant didn't have enough of an action look, so I created a new vision and had my architectural firm do a second rendering, this time capturing a *Dukes of Hazard* feel. There was still a problem; it just wasn't there yet. I decided I didn't want to go with a "peanuts on the floor, hot rod out the door" look . . . I wanted something more.

At about this time, I became fascinated with a new cable show, *American Choppers*, which focused on a father and his sons who built the custom motorcycle business Orange County Choppers. I thought it would be great to feature this concept in my new restaurant. The OCC theme seemed to go better with a more art deco, sleek, hip look, which, I believed, would appeal to young and old patrons alike. At the same time, I decided the restaurant needed a name makeover and we went with Backfire BBQ: Bikes, Burgers and BBQ featuring Orange County Choppers. In our designs, we highlighted the stars of the television show on the front of the restaurant, along with the motorcycle insignia of the Orange County Choppers and a listing of a few menu items to be found inside the restaurant.

What makes this whole process so interesting was that, at each step in the process, I could have decided the restaurant of the moment was *it* and finalized the design. Yet, by not making a snap decision, by allowing enough time to let the creative process work, by being willing to make improvements when the possibility of incorporating Orange County Choppers presented itself, and, finally, by getting other creative people involved and competing to present the best possible product, we were able to create a themed-restaurant concept that was far superior to what it started out to be.

In addition to making improvements in your decisions before implementing them it's also important to encourage others to feel free to check your creative vision. This proved to be crucial during the marketing of the T-Rex restaurant. As an opening-day gimmick, I had thought it would be a clever idea to have a huge animatronic T-Rex dinosaur placed right outside the entrance to the restaurant and program it to pick up a child (a paid actor) in its mouth, transport him over a low wall separating the establishment from the parking lot, and deposit him at the restaurant's front door. My staff was *horrified* at the idea and rightfully pointed out what I had inexplicably overlooked: that five hundred kids waiting in line to eat would probably run hysterically into the street, never to be coaxed back again! If I ever doubted the importance of allowing adequate time to incubate creative concepts before implementing them, the T-Rex child-transport idea banished those doubts forever.

Making Improvements after Marketing Your Product or Service

I have an entrepreneurial friend who once told me, "Steve, once my product is out there for public consumption, I'm done with it. It's time to move on." It's disheartening to see that many entrepreneurs share his belief: create it, sell it, and forget about it.

Such an attitude astounds me. I liken it to the parent who, upon sending her children out into the world, detaches from their lives. I'm certainly not suggesting that entrepreneurs become fixated on what they have produced, following what happens to each creation to the exclusion of pursuing any new ideas. However, I do think it is helpful—and sound business practice— to evaluate products and/or services you create once they've been on the market for a while. It is often the case that glitches and problems with specific products and services become apparent only *after* they have been available in the marketplace. It is at these times that unanticipated difficulties and unexpected results can arise: difficulties and results that could not be anticipated in the formulation (or even the testing) of the products or services before being made available for general consumption.

This, too, is a lesson I've learned through my own entre-preneurial experience: unanticipated problems can arise after a product is put into circulation; what matters is how you take care of them.

In 2006, we opened the Yak & Yeti restaurant at Disney's Animal Kingdom. A family-friendly, Asian-inspired restaurant, it was divided into two parts: a sit-down indoor area and an outdoor walk-up window. One of the advertised benefits of the walk-up window was the opportunity to get faster service.

Several months after Yak & Yeti opened, I stopped by to see how things were going. I took a seat outside, near the "quick service" outdoor section of the restaurant, and noticed people having to wait in line for up to fifteen minutes to place their food orders. In my mind, this was a substantial problem, and what made things even worse was the realization that an obvious solution to the problem existed, yet none of the staff had either seen the problem or had chosen to correct it in the eight months the restaurant had been in operation.

The problem involved the placement of the menu boards customers used to make their food selections. They were on signs behind the serving counter, so that the patrons had to get close to the front of the line before they could see what items were on the menu. This gave them precious little time to make their choices, meaning that when they reached the employee taking their orders, they weren't ready to announce their selections. This, of course, delayed everything as the employee waited patiently for the customers to make their decisions. The way to fix the problem was simple enough: additional menu boards had to be posted farther back along the sidewalk where the customers were lined up. That way, people positioned at the back of the line would have more time to make their decisions and, when they got to the front of the line, would be ready to place their order without further delay, speeding everything up significantly.

How can a restaurant advertising quick service expect to make significant money when people have to wait two or three times as long as necessary to get their meals? It can't, and that is why it is important to monitor what services or products you have provided: to make sure things are going smoothly, and, if not, to make the necessary improvements to ensure that they do.

Remember: whether it involves making improvements before and/or after you market your product or service, you should never stop assessing, enhancing, and learning all you can about your creations. It is this knowledge that can help you get ahead and stay ahead. My grandfather used to say, "You learn, and you learn, and you learn, and then you die . . . and when you stop learning, you start dying. So, if you ever think you know it all, you're on your way out."

Keep learning! Stay in the game. That way you'll be in a great position to win once you take the field, and keep winning every time you return to the scene of your triumph.

CHAPTER 12

On Marketing: Customers Won't Buy What They Don't Know Exists

Self-examination Question:
Is marketing a significant part of
your entrepreneurial plan?

One of my friends is a writer with a bad attitude. Recently, he had his manuscript accepted by a New York publisher and nine months later the book hit the stores. In an attempt to boost sales, the publisher's marketing department asked my friend to help push the book by doing some interviews and bookstore appearances. He refused, claiming that it was "beneath his dignity" to "peddle his work." As far as he was concerned, his job was to write the book and the publisher's job was to sell it.

That's what I mean by a "bad attitude." Maybe if you're a John Grisham or a J. K. Rowling, you can get away with birthing your book and then letting others raise it to marketplace success, but, in the real world where most of us entrepreneurs and independent contractors do our work, taking a personal role in marketing your product effectively is sometimes as important as creating the product itself.

I never, ever miss an opportunity to market my creations. Success or failure isn't always determined by the quality of what you produce or provide; it is also a function of public awareness that your product or service is out there and available for purchase.

I remember receiving a call early in my career from a magazine writer who wanted to do a feature story on our new themed restaurant, Juke Box Saturday Night. I jumped at the chance for the publicity. Actually, I *flew* at the chance. I hopped on a plane from Chicago to Los Angeles the very next day, in order to meet with the journalist who wanted to interview me. I ended up with a major article on my restaurant appearing in *Entrepreneur* magazine. As a matter of fact, it became the cover story. Would that have happened if I simply did a phone interview from Chicago and didn't fly out to Los Angeles?

Probably not.

What if I hadn't responded to the writer at all?

A total loss of valuable publicity.

There are some people who believe that I spend as much of my creative energy figuring out how to market our ideas as I do creating them. I don't think that's true, but I certainly recognize the importance of marketing for achieving success, and so should you. Of course, some entrepreneurial undertakings are more easily marketable than others. They provide more angles to exploit. But, generally, I believe almost any entrepreneurial product can be marketed if the businessperson involved is willing to use imagination and expend effort to gain public awareness and media attention.

When I was running the Minneapolis location of Juke Box Saturday Night, I was always thinking up publicity stunts to bring more business to the club. One time, when the Minnesota Twins were in the World Series, I offered to clean each fan's "Homer Hanky" (fans twirled them over their heads during the game) outside my establishment. I arranged with the owner of the dry-cleaning service across the street to set up a row of machines outside Juke Box where we created an assembly line–style cleaning process. Thousands of fans got their hankies cleaned and pressed. They loved it. It created a lot of goodwill. Of course, a lot of the fans, proudly sporting their spotless hankies, then stepped into our restaurant, spent money, and swelled our bottom line. On top of that we got free, extensive radio, television, and domestic and international newspaper coverage of the stunt—far more publicity for our establishment than we ever could have afforded with our limited advertising budget.

When the Twins won the World Series in 1987, we got another shot at a marketing coup. Paul Ridgeway, the big-time event planner in charge of organizing the victory parade, called me and said, "I heard you're from New York and wondered what kind of parade a Manhattan guy would throw." I suggested a ticker-tape parade—an idea he accepted and quickly put me in charge of. So I planned the ticker-tape parade, but with a twist: the ticker tape wouldn't be paper confetti; it would be money, millions of dollars of shredded U.S. currency!

Everyone bought into the idea. Now all I had to do was get the money: $10 million worth, to be precise. I checked with several local banks, the FBI, and even the CIA. They thought it was the craziest idea they ever heard, but directed me to the Federal Reserve Bank in Minnesota. The people there were much more positive about the plan. They had to take old money out of circulation and destroy it anyway, so it wasn't much of a stretch to chop the cash into confetti-size pieces and send boxes of the stuff in a Federal Reserve truck directly to my restaurant. The Federal Reserve Bank didn't charge us a cent; I guessed they loved the Twins, too. We tossed all the confetti-cash into a rented dumpster and announced we were giving away millions of shredded dollars to use in the parade. People began lining up at seven o'clock in the morning and waited hours for a chance to scoop out their share of the booty into paper bags. We gave out a stash of cash to thousands of families. The PR we got out of that idea was worth well over a million dollars: the story of the "confetti-cash" ticker-tape parade made the front pages of both *USA Today* and *The New York Times*.

The confetti-cash parade demonstrates how marketing your product can be profitable and fun: Juke Box got a bottom-line boost from the event and everyone had a good time in the process. (Well, *almost* everyone. It turns out that the Federal Reserve banking system got thousands of additional requests for "confetti-cash" after our parade and the institution vowed never to give out shredded money again. From what I understand, it has kept that promise to this day.)

As far as I'm concerned, the boundaries of my marketing efforts are the limits of my imagination. I always challenge myself to find new and impactful ways to attract attention to my product, and I make the process fun. You can, too. Once you incorporate the marketing function of your product or service into your overall plan for entrepreneurial success, you'll find yourself getting more enthusiastic and excited about generating publicity.

This enthusiasm can lead to some wild and crazy stunts. One time, I was slated to address a gathering of reporters and business leaders about the advantages of Backfire BBQ, our Orange County Choppers–themed restaurant. Everyone was seated in a large tent near the proposed construction site. When it was my turn to speak, heads turned and people stared. I came roaring up on a hundred-decibel, custom-built motorcycle, wearing a fancy suit, shiny Italian loafers, and a big grin on my face. The photo of my entrance made all the newspapers and turned a humdrum conference into a media-worthy event.

Another time we were scheduled to do a groundbreaking for our T-Rex dinosaur restaurant in Kansas City. Usually, such an event involves a few dignitaries breaking ground with gold-plated shovels. I decided to spice things up. The night before the ceremony was to take place, we buried some replicas of dinosaur bones and a large T-Rex skeletal head in the ground. The next day, with press gathered around, the chosen movers and shakers turned the earth with their gold shovels . . . and "discovered" dinosaur bones. Meanwhile, the mayor, who was sitting atop a backhoe, plunged the scoop into the ground and pulled out the huge T-Rex dinosaur head. Everyone laughed, and the scene played out as the featured story on the evening news and the front page of the newspaper.

One marketing principle I always observe when trying to sell my ideas is that, if the customer can't come to you, you go to the customer. For some entrepreneurs, this is not a difficult task; all they have to do is show up with a briefcase full of papers or a computer disc with a PowerPoint presentation. With some of my creations, going to the customer takes on a whole new meaning.

When we first began pitching our T-Rex concept, we were interested in selling the concept to the Simon Property Group. The executives weren't able to visit our warehouse display in Golden Valley, Minnesota, but they were willing to see what we had to offer if we came to their headquarters, located on the upper floors of the Hyatt Hotel in downtown Indianapolis, Indiana. The question was: how could we set up our display for the executives to see?

The answer: a floor show.

I met with the general manager of the Hyatt Hotel and we agreed upon a plan. I would unload four twenty-eight-foot semi trucks packed with faux dinosaurs and associated props inside his lobby. I would decorate the entire area to look like a prehistoric jungle, and get the whole job done between six o'clock in the evening and six o'clock the next morning. Because the dinosaurs were so big, we couldn't simply cart them in the front door. We had to hire a team of glass-company employees to pull the plate-glass windows out of the front of the hotel so we could fit the dinos into the hotel lobby and then put the glass back in place. The glass-removal process had to be repeated once we were ready to pack up and leave. It was quite a scene, with a row of glass-company trucks stacked up outside the Hyatt and a bunch of guys pulling out windows and hauling dinosaurs into the lobby of the hotel. It cost us $35,000 just to get the show set up.

The next morning, as the executives of Simon Property Group walked through the lobby I'd transformed into a jungle, they were blown away. They had never seen a creative sales presentation like that. And we ended up with a deal.

Another time we rented a convoy of trucks and headed to Orlando to show Disney our T-Rex concept. This was an even bigger effort than the Indianapolis trip. We had dozens of dinos ready for showing. Our enthusiasm was over the top, but our timing was lousy. The day we targeted to give our demonstration was September 11, 2001. After what happened in New York City, nobody was in any kind of mood to see a presentation. It was a sad day for us, but a far sadder day for our country.

It was at this point that David Siegel stepped in and saved the day. David is a wonderful friend and leading time-share developer based in Florida. He was gracious enough to give us permission to set up our display for a week in the ballroom of his Westgate Resort, about five miles from Disney. What started as a weeklong occupancy ended up as an eight-month odyssey. It took that long to get the Disney people, still reeling from one of the most devastating events in the history of our country, to check out our project and eventually get on board with the idea.

Marketing your product or service can be fun, and it can

also be challenging. I never miss an opportunity to show our ideas. For that reason, I used to carry a working model of the T-Rex restaurant in the back of my car. The model was about four-by-four feet and cost thousands of dollars to build. But it was there when I needed it, always available for a spontaneous showing. I remember many a lunch or dinner with a potential investor where the topic of the restaurant would come up and the investor would say, "I'd really like to see that someday." I smiled, and at the end of the meal I led the person out to my car, popped the trunk, and—presto!—a portable T-Rex was there for the observing.

I never stop selling our ideas. I'm always thinking of new ways to promote what we're doing. If someone wants to see my projects, I want to be ready to go on with the show . . . because it might be the only chance I get to pitch that investor. That means I'm always ready and willing to market my ideas. You should be, too.

CHAPTER 13

Budget, Don't Begrudge It

Self-examination Question:
Do you give proper attention to
keeping within budget when completing
your projects?

ntrepreneurs and budgets don't always mix well. One
venture capitalist proposed this tongue-in-cheek formula
for determining entrepreneurial cost overruns:

$$PC = OBM + IRBB$$
$$where$$
$$PC = Project\ Cost$$
$$OBM = Original\ Budgeted\ Money$$
$$and$$
$$IRBB = Investorís\ Remaining\ Bank\ Balance$$

Of course, this is a joke (entrepreneurs are not solely out to
break the bank), yet it is a well-documented fact that projects
seem to come in well over budget with disturbing regularity.

Budget overruns can create tension between entrepreneurs
and their backers. They should be avoided whenever possible.
My most memorable experience with going over budget (sadly,
not the first—and certainly not the last) happened during the
construction of our first Rainforest Cafe at the Mall of America
and involved Lyle Berman, the venture capitalist who backed the
project from the outset.

At the time, the restaurant was close to completion, which
was the good news, but the bad news was that I was a million
dollars over budget. When I called Lyle to tell him, he was—to
put it lightly—unhappy. "How can you be fifty percent over
budget?" he wailed, asking a question I sensed he didn't really
want answered, because he didn't wait for a reply.

"Listen, Steve," he said, inhaling sharply. "I want you to take
the rest of the day off and enjoy yourself. Have you seen the
movie *Bugsy*?"

"No," I replied.

"Well, I want you to promise me you'll go rent a copy and watch it tonight."

"Why that particular movie?" I asked.

"Just do it," Lyle answered and hung up the phone.

That evening, I got the film . . . and I also got the message. For those of you who didn't see the movie, Benjamin Siegel, the main character in the film, is murdered for going over budget in building his lavish Las Vegas casino. Of course, Lyle was joking (I hope) but I was much more careful about coming in at or near budget from that point on!

Budgie vs. Budget

One problem entrepreneurs have when it comes to budget considerations is the clash between what they think must be spent to make their idea work and the amount of money the investors believe is sufficient to bring the project to market. For example, one of the main attractions of the original Rain Forest Cafes—and a major reason I built them—was to highlight the beautiful parrots that inhabited the real rain forests of the world. My love affair with these creatures began when I was a teenager and got my first scarlet macaw, named Jules (after my father), which is still alive and lives with me to this day. I felt that these beautiful creatures would not only add to the authenticity of the rainforest dining experience but also encourage people to appreciate the birds and help promote their preservation around the world.

Keeping the birds in each restaurant was not cheap. Before we came along, no tropical birds had been allowed around food, for reasons of food safety. To get permission to put them in the restaurant I ended up working with the health department—both local and federal officials—to invent an air filtration and purification system that took the spurs of birds out of the air. That cost money. So did the eight-hundred-square-foot habitat room where the birds were kept when not on display in the restaurant. Then there was the cost of feeding the birds and paying trained people (a curator with several assistants) to look after the birds' health and welfare. All in all, it cost about $100,000 per year to keep the birds in each Rainforest Cafe.

When the Rainforest Cafe chain was sold to Landry's in 2000, it was decided that when it came to birds versus bucks, the parrots were an excessive cost, and they were removed from the restaurants. Of course, I didn't agree with Landry's decision. I felt the marketing value of the birds alone justified their cost, but I was overruled. As an entrepreneur—unless you cover all the costs to create, market, and sell your own product or service—you need to recognize that those who foot the bill for bringing your product or service to market have some say in how and where that money should be spent. *How* much say they have should be clearly spelled out in advance of going forward with any business deal to avoid hard feelings and, worse, potential legal challenges down the road.

Drove My Chevy to the Levy, But the Levy Was High

I have come to believe that there will always be some budget tension between creative entrepreneurs who want to present their perfect innovative vision, and pragmatic business investors who want to get the highest return on their investment. Back in my Juke Box Saturday Night days, I had wanted to find a 1957 Chevy to cut in half, using the front end to stick outside the building, with it actually coming out the front wall. I told my partner, Jimmy Rittenberg, about the idea and said it would cost a few grand to buy the car.

Jimmy said, "A few grand? Why not buy a '50 Ford and cut it up? You can get one of those for nine hundred bucks."

I replied, "It's not the same."

He argued, "What do you mean, it's not the same? It's the front end of a car."

I countered, "It's not the front end of a '57 Chevy. What you don't understand is the '57 Chevy exemplifies the fifties and sixties, what we're trying to create here. When you look at a '57 Chevy, the car smiles at you. When you look at a '50 Ford it says, 'Screw you.' When you look at a '57 Chevy, it says 'ALL RIGHT!'"

I finally got the money, but it was a tense situation and uncomfortable, too. Beauty is in the eye of the beholder. Creative decisions are not always reached by consensus.

The longer I have pursued the entrepreneurial life, the more convinced I have become that the best way to handle budget problems is to keep them from happening in the first place. This feat is best accomplished when both the investor and the entrepreneur are on the same page when it comes to understanding what a project will cost and how the money should be allocated. Have those important conversations about cost and vision early, and make sure you have them often.

CHAPTER 14

Don't Be Afraid to Develop Strategic Partnerships

Self-examination Question:
When you develop a product or service, do you consider forging strategic alliances with other established businesses to help market and/or sell your creation more successfully?

When I asked a group of students to pick some words or phrases they thought described entrepreneurs, one of the common responses was "lone wolf." It is an apt label, as many entrepreneurs do choose to work alone, to toil independently in search of a product or service that will bring them financial success. To a certain degree, the magnitude of a project will be a factor in how easy it is to go it alone in bringing that product or service to market. But for projects big or small, what an entrepreneur should avoid doing is reinventing the wheel.

It is a waste of time and resources to undertake this duplication of effort and, often, the wheel that is already out there is better than the one the entrepreneur creates. This is where the development of strategic partnerships comes into play.

Here is a case in point. All of our restaurants have a retail component, a store within the establishment that sells products related to the theme of the restaurant. Our new T-Rex chain of restaurants was no exception, so we decided to sell plush dinosaur toys in our retail outlet. We thought it would be great if young visitors to the restaurant could build their own dinosaurs from a selection of various body shapes, colors, and clothing. In fact, a company already existed that used this idea, but with bears rather than dinosaurs. It was called Build-A-Bear Workshop, and it was successfully operating in malls throughout America.

We could have attempted to duplicate what Build-A-Bear had already achieved, but why? They had an excellent product, so why spend time re-creating what is already available? We decided it was smarter to join forces with a business that already offered a superior product than to spend unnecessary time and money trying to prove we could do the same thing. Build-A-Bear had already researched the product, had the factories and the means to produce what was needed, and had an established reputation as a great retailer and promoter.

I contacted Maxine Clark, the dynamic brains behind Build-A-Bear, and suggested a strategic alliance between our company and hers. She agreed to spend half a million dollars to retool her operation so she could create a Build-A-Dino retail outlet in our T-Rex establishments; both of our companies would profit from the sales. It was an instant success. Approximately 25 percent of our total restaurant sales comes from our retail operations, and, at T-Rex, 50 percent of all retail sales comes from one product: Build-A-Dino. A business relationship between my organization and Maxine Clark's Build-A-Bear is a classic example of a win-win business situation where two companies form a strategic partnership that avoids duplication of effort, saves time, enhances marketing potential, and makes money for all concerned.

Probably my most unique partnering agreement involved Budweiser. I got the local Budweiser distributor's agreement to help sponsor construction of a giant mural depicting King Kong climbing the wall of our Juke Box Saturday Night club and restaurant in Minneapolis. The artwork included a real Cessna 150 airplane coming out of the wall and an actual helicopter parked on the roof of the building directly over our front entrance. The chimney of the building became the Budweiser beer can that King Kong was holding.

This mural was so popular with the city and the public that we later convinced the family that owned an adjacent building across the parking lot to allow our mural artist to paint a second rendering, this time of the Wizard of Oz. We convinced Royal Crown Cola International, manufacturers of RC Cola, to sponsor that mural.

There was an outdoor space between the King Kong mural on our building and the Wizard of Oz mural on the building across the parking lot. We did not own that space, but—given the popularity of both pieces of artwork—we often got permission from the city to stage outdoor events for hundreds of people in that area. This was to our advantage, as it increased the volume of customers we served and had a direct positive impact on the bottom line of the restaurant and club.

This is the value of strategic relationship building. Those murals and our strategic relationships with the vendors and our neighbors spanned seven successful years. We ended up with an eye-catching gimmick that generated publicity and profits for Juke Box. When was the last time you heard of a soda and a beer company working together?

The point is that there are many times that, with a little creative thinking, you can come up with strategic partnerships to facilitate the creation of a product or service, enhance its quality, and improve your profit margin at the same time. Lone wolves have their place in the entrepreneurial scheme of things, but, sometimes, given the choice, it's better to run with a professional, well-vetted pack than to go it alone.

CHAPTER 15

Marketing Yourself to Market Your Product

Self-examination Question:
Do you consider (and take advantage
of) the impact you have when selling
your idea, product, or service?

Many years ago I agreed to attend a Broadway show with a friend from New York. I don't remember the name of the show, but I vividly recall my friend's reaction when he discovered the actor in the lead role was sick and would be replaced by an understudy.

"Let's get out of here," he said firmly.

"Why?" I protested, "We already paid for the tickets and we've got good seats."

"I came to see the actor who is sick."

"But the show's still going on," I said. "Besides, the understudy might be just as good."

My friend was resolute. "I came here to see the main actor, not some backup," he huffed. "I don't want to see the play without him." And with that, he got up, motioned me to follow, and walked out of the theater.

Now, here's what I find interesting: there are many venture capitalists and investors who feel about entrepreneurs the way my friend felt about the actor in the play—they don't want to go on with the show unless it's with the specific entrepreneur in whom they have invested. In other words, the person committing his money to a project is as concerned (or more concerned) with who is heading up the project as he is with the project itself.

For this reason, it is critically important that aspiring and established entrepreneurs keep in mind that success in convincing investors to back your project will always be based on two things: (1) their perceived viability of your idea and (2) their impression of you. In other words, when it comes to entrepreneurial success you need to be able to sell your product and/or service and be able to sell yourself as well.

Think about it. If someone came up to you and said, "Will you back me with cold, hard cash?" what factors would you consider in making your decision? You would assess the commercial value of what the entrepreneur was proposing, but you wouldn't stop there. You'd also be interested in that person's commitment to her idea, her sense of dedication to what she was proposing, and the "sweat equity" she was willing to invest in making her dream a reality.

Now I'm not suggesting that all entrepreneurs have to go so far as turn their houses into rainforests or load up warehouses full of dinosaurs to show investors they are committed to their idea. But immersing yourself in your concept or idea certainly tells a potential investor you're committed to achieving your objective. After all, investors are risking their money on you; they want to know you have something at stake as well.

"How committed are you to your idea?" I can't tell you how often investors have asked me this question. After seeing my rainforest house, some investors thought I should be committed—not to my idea but to an institution! But when they saw what I was willing to do to make my idea work, they were impressed. They saw the raw ambition, passion, and enthusiasm. They saw my level of commitment and it gave them a reason to invest. When someone shows true passion and enthusiasm for an idea, it makes people want to be part of the vision and makes them more convinced the idea will succeed, that their financial investment will reap significant dividends.

If you don't believe strongly in your idea, who else will? If you don't show enthusiasm and dedication to your idea, why would anyone else get excited about its chances for ultimate success? If you don't stand behind your idea with a commitment to labor vigorously to see it become reality, what kind of person would offer financial backing to see it through to completion?

Investors want you to have "skin" in the game.

Go out there and sell your idea, or your product, or your service, but don't forget: you also need to sell yourself. How strongly do I feel about this? Strongly enough to unequivocally state that promotion is a central focus of my life. I believe that the day you stop promoting yourself is the day you die.

Making a Good First Impression Is Critical

In a perfect world, new entrepreneurs going out with their first idea would make just one appointment with a venture capitalist who would immediately agree to provide as much cash as needed to make the idea a reality. If only it were so! Seasoned entrepreneurs, even the successful ones, know that rejections and desperate scrambles for financial resources are the rule rather than the exception in the contemporary business world.

It's tough to get people to give you their money, but you can increase your chances of success if you present yourself to potential investors in the appropriate manner. You need to behave and dress in a manner that will enhance your credibility and, in turn, increase the probability an investor will take you seriously enough to consider risking money on your idea. This is particularly important the first time you meet a prospective investor, because first impressions are often lasting impressions and color any interactions that follow.

Behavioral scientists have identified things you can do to make a positive impression on people you want to influence, focusing on such things as dress and nonverbal behaviors to enhance your interpersonal success with others. Some techniques work better than others. I used to assume that any thinking individual would practice these techniques because they were common sense. Sadly, common sense doesn't always translate into common practice and I am amazed at how many otherwise intelligent and creative individuals fail to practice the most rudimentary steps in establishing a good first impression. Add to this the fact that many articles and books have been written on the topic of establishing good first impressions, and it becomes even more astounding that would-be entrepreneurs don't follow established and well-known procedures for impressing potential clients. Thus, I find it necessary to mention these recommendations for making a positive first impression an additional time in these pages. They really do make a difference in gaining the confidence and cash of clients whom you look to for support of your project.

Physical Appearance

There's an old saying that "clothes make the man." (In today's world, we would want to include women in that statement and recognize that it is still as valid today as when it was first spoken.) I always make it a practice to wear a suit when I'm meeting with investors or attending business meetings where my projects are discussed. That includes visits to Florida, where people often say I'm overdressed because it's hot in the Sunshine State and many people just wear collared shirts at work.

I don't agree with them. I think a suit (or a comparable formal outfit for women) is mandatory apparel for a first meeting with a customer, client, and/or investor. When I visited the Disney Imagineering Department I wore a suit. I felt it showed respect for the people I was meeting. It's a bit like the newscaster who told me why he wore makeup to cover up the dark circles under his eyes when he was on the set. "I'm in people's living rooms for a half hour or more," he said. "I owe it to them to look my best." He's got a point. I don't think you can be too overdressed, but you can end up underdressed. Why take the risk?

Physical appearance also involves the way you groom yourself, even the way you smell. It does no good to wear a carefully crafted suit or dress and then show up with hair coming out of your ears and nose. Dirty hair and unkempt beards are also a no-no, along with scraggly nails, bad breath, body odor, or the use of too much cologne or perfume.

The Handshake

The handshake is a critical part of most first meetings with potential investors. If you do it incorrectly, it might be the only time it happens. If you do it right, it increases the chances you'll shake hands again when you close your deal.

Nobody likes a wet handshake. It turns people off. If you have sweaty palms, make certain you wipe them off so they're dry before you attempt to shake hands. Limp handshakes aren't recommended, either. A firm grip is preferable. Have your thumb go inside the thumb of the hand you are shaking. Never grab the end of someone's hand, as it can be perceived as offensive. Also, recognize that a handshake is an acceptable means of greeting, not a wrestling contest. The grip should be firm, but shouldn't be bone-crushing. Additionally, pay attention to the length of the shake, and take care not to shake too long. It's a handshake, after all, not a finger embrace.

Body Language

Joe Navarro, highly respected body-language expert and coauthor of *What Every BODY Is Saying: An Ex-FBI Agent's Guide to Speed-Reading People,* points out that 60–70 percent of all communication is nonverbal. With those kinds of numbers, you can see why physical gestures play a critical role in determining the overall success of your interactions with others. You need to be aware of the body language you are giving off for others to see. Your facial expressions are particularly critical. Looking indifferent, hostile, or displeased will not sit well with someone you want to impress. Don't roll your eyes, sneer, tighten your jaw, or compress your lips. These nonverbal behaviors will often be interpreted negatively by the person who sees them. A display of friendliness, a well-timed smile, and appropriate eye contact (not too long, but made on a regular basis during a meeting) will create a more positive atmosphere, as will good posture (alert and upright, not slouching or leaning away) and attentiveness (looking all over the room sends a message of disinterest and will not be well received).

Try to remain calm and interested throughout your meeting. Pay attention to what your potential investor has to say; don't constantly interrupt or give short shrift to his questions. Listening carefully not only shows respect for the speaker, but will also allow you to gain a better understanding of what he wants. Bobbing your head up and down gently while the other person speaks and/or tilting your head to one side also facilitates communication and sends out a nonverbal message that you have a receptive attitude toward what is being said.

Leave Something Behind That People Will Remember You By

Each time I meet a new person, that individual could be a potential investor or someone who might provide assistance to me in some way. Sometimes these meetings are planned, like when a person visits my warehouse for a tour, but often they're not, like a chance encounter with a businessperson assigned to the seat next to mine on a cross-country flight. At the end of these interactions, I always want to leave the person with something special that will make me memorable in her mind. I want to give her something that will help jog her memory about who I am, should I need to call her or work with her sometime in the future. I want her to have something that represents me as a creative entrepreneur and helps set me apart from all the other business contacts people make in their lifetimes.

What might that something be?

An item that few people think about, but which I have developed as a major marketing tool in my entrepreneurial endeavors, is the business card.

The business card. It's either the first or last thing you give to people when meeting them. It's also the item by which you are remembered, should the person who received the card have reason to use it in the future. I decided to develop a business card that had legs.

I created my first unique business card in the mid-1980s, a plastic card in the shape of a 1957 Chevy convertible. When I first came up with the idea for the card, my partners thought I was crazy. The business cards cost twenty-five cents apiece, a huge chunk of change in those days. But it was made of plastic, so it was indestructible—you could spill drinks on it, you could bend it, but you couldn't break it. Every Juke Box Saturday Night club and restaurant I owned at that time had a '57 Chevy sticking out the front wall, and I drove a restored '57 Chevy, so it turned out that the item was more than just a business card; it was a reflection of my personality. In fact, my business card *was* me.

The card ended up generating far more publicity and attention for our club than it cost to produce. The card was featured in *Inc.* magazine and the *Detroit News,* and people still keep the card even though the club has been closed for decades. Business card collectors called me to acquire them and quite often I would get calls from guests requesting "one of those cool business cards."

I have continued to create unique business cards as a way of setting myself and my business apart from the competition with each new themed attraction, restaurant, and retail store we open. I'm always working to develop a card that says "WOW!" when a person receives it. I figure if we claim to be innovative and creative, then our cards better reflect that claim.

I have spent hundreds of hours and gone through dozens of card designs before getting it right and settling on a card I'm satisfied with. Sometimes the type is too small, sometimes the logo seems wrong, or the colors aren't perfect. Sometimes the card is too large or too small, or the shape isn't quite right. But, eventually, I am able to produce a business card that captures who I am as a person, what our team is as a company, and why we are something special. The cards are expensive, but, as I indicated earlier, people don't forget us when they receive one of our business cards. Oftentimes, they will put the card in a prominent place and refer to it in conversations with others.

As an entrepreneur, you might want to consider designing a special business card to capture the attention of your prospective investors. I would also recommend that you develop a telephone answering system that is memorable and unique, so when people call your business they don't get dead air or canned music, but rather learn innovative, useful information about what you can do, are doing, or have done. The important thing is to set yourself apart from the crowd, to give people something by which to remember you. (See Chapter 24 for more on this subject.)

The recorded voice on your telephone message should be upbeat and infectious. Having an engaging voice is sometimes as important as the content of the message. Produce an effective phone message and you'll be giving yourself a valuable entrepreneurial edge over your competition.

There are a few crucial moments in setting impressions, so it's essential to be aware of each of those make-or-break opportunities. By taking care in the way you present yourself and your business to others, you can effectively set the tone and tenor for a potential investor's entire opinion of you. It's essential to always remember that the critical first impression can often be what seals the deal.

SECTION III
PERSISTENCE

CHAPTER 16

Persist and Prevail

"A diamond is a lump of coal that stuck with it."

—Anonymous

Self-examination Question:
Do you give up easily or are you
willing to pursue your goals with
tenacity and determination?

Many of us dream, yet few of us achieve our dreams. Why? Sadly, it is often because we give up too easily. We accept one setback as total defeat, break off our pursuit of a goal because we lack the mental toughness to keep going. If only we had the determination to stay the course, to persist in our quest for success. One man had such a dream and he lived to realize it *because* he dedicated his life to realizing it. Consider what he went through.

> He failed in business in 1831.
> He was defeated for the legislature in 1832.
> He had a second business bankruptcy in 1833.
> He suffered a nervous breakdown in 1836.
> He was defeated for speaker of the Illinois house in 1838.
> He was defeated for elector of the Illinois senate in 1840.
> He was defeated for the U.S. Congress in 1843.
> He was again defeated for the U.S. Congress in 1848.
> He was defeated for the U.S. Senate in 1855.
> He was defeated for the U.S. vice presidency in 1856.
> He was defeated a second time for the U.S. Senate in 1858.
> He was elected president of the United States of America in 1860.

Would you have had the persistence to stay the course after taking so many risks and failing so many times? Not many people would. But, as Abraham Lincoln found out, persistence pays. A century after Lincoln's inauguration, baseball great Tommy

Lasorda would elegantly describe what "Honest Abe" had discovered: "The difference between the impossible and the possible lies in a person's determination."

In my own life, I've always been a "never say die" kind of guy. If I took on a task, I just never wanted to quit until I achieved my objective. I always believed that if I tried hard enough and long enough, I'd prevail. I remember once in high school my coach sent me into a basketball game to try and stop the opposing team's highest scorer, who was just killing us. I wasn't much of a basketball player since I was too short, but I could jump high for rebounds. And what I lacked in height, I made up for in tenacity.

I remember hounding my opponent at every move. I was in his face, bound and determined he wouldn't get the ball or, if he did, that he wouldn't get a clear shot no matter what. I was *determined* to keep him from scoring. I was like a bulldog, the annoying, relentless kind that doesn't let you move anywhere without being on your case.

I guess my opponent wasn't used to being guarded by someone with such a fierce desire to do his job with such persistence. He got so mad that he threw the ball at me and got kicked out of the game for unsportsmanlike conduct. Mind you, I never fouled the guy or did anything illegal; I just persisted with all my energy, and when a person persists with all his heart he usually gets results.

When I was in radio and television sales, I utilized the persist-and-prevail philosophy to get jobs. I already mentioned my Superman story as one example in an earlier chapter. I'd like to add one additional comment about that experience here, as it has to do with perseverance in the face of potential failure.

At several points during my trip to the station manager's office, things went wrong, and I could have become discouraged while jammed into that crate and just climbed out and scuttled the plan. I guess you could call it my "Kryptonite Moment." I could have succumbed. But I didn't. I persisted. I played the hand I was dealt. I didn't give up. Even when faced with potential humiliation—stinking of rancid meat, hair matted with Diet Coke, my Superman outfit stained with particles of salami and pickle—I went on with the show.

When the lid came off that barrel, I could have stood up and apologized, asked for a doctor, and slunk off in embarrassment. But that isn't my style. Life isn't always scripted. You have to play with what you have, go with the flow. At the end of the day, those who succeed are those who are flexible and can adapt to unanticipated circumstances, and even turn unexpected situations to their advantage. What's most important is that they are capable of persisting in the face of adversity.

I learned that lesson well when my superhero persistence paid off with a job offer. It was lesson I recalled when it was time to find my next position.

I wanted a position in television sales, so I contacted a top agency in New York City. I decided to send the chairman of the board my resume and to do it in a manner that would catch his attention and get me noticed. I purchased a huge toy boat—one about four feet long with three smokestacks that looked like a passenger cruise ship. (This was not the kind of vessel you'd play with in the bathtub; there'd be no room for any water.)

I put my resume in the boat, put the boat in a large box, and had it shipped to the chairman via special delivery. I figured that it would be the first resume he ever received that arrived in a boat. Along with the resume I enclosed a letter that concluded with "Please welcome me aboard."

About a week later, I got the boat back in the mail, along with my resume and a reply which said, "Your boat has leaks in it, but keep trying."

Well, needless to say, those words were just the challenge a persistent person loves to hear. I purchased some miniature life preservers, attached them to the boat along with my resume and a new letter, and shipped the whole thing back to the chairman. The letter said, "I'm your life preserver. Welcome me aboard and your boat will float again."

That got me a plane ticket to New York, an interview, and the job.

I was determined and persistent when it came to romance, too. Once I'd met the girl I wanted to marry and was ready to pop the question, I wanted the best chance of getting an affirmative response, so I decided to create a romantic setting with a little help from my friends in Florida. I rented out the Magic Kingdom at Walt Disney World (yes, the entire park) and put my plan into action.

Just before the park officially closed to the public for the night, my girlfriend and I were eating dinner at one of Disney's restaurants when the waiter (who was in on the scheme) told me I had an important call. When I left the table to take the call (there were no cell phones in those days), a Disney character, dressed as Major Domo, approached my girlfriend and said, "Please follow me." She hesitated but did as she was told, walking out to the street where a coachman, dressed in tights, a wig, and a tricorn hat, stood next to Cinderella's lavishly decorated carriage, pulled by twelve white horses.

Major Domo told my girlfriend to get in the carriage. As she tried to figure out exactly what was happening, the coachman drove her through the entire Magic Kingdom. Even though the park was now closed, all the lights remained on, and music was playing everywhere. The coachman pulled alongside the Cinderella Castle and stopped. Major Domo helped my date step down from her seat and there, against the backdrop of the castle, stood Mickey, Minnie, Donald, and all the other Disney characters lined up waiting to greet her. A six-piece band was playing in the background.

At that moment, from the other end of Main Street, I came to my "princess" astride a large white stallion. I was dressed in a Prince Charming outfit and carried a glass slipper in one hand. I rode up to my lady, dismounted, and, bowing down on one knee, carefully placed the slipper on her foot (it fit!) and took a ring from my pocket.

That's when I asked her to marry me. Fortunately, she said yes, and, the moment the words came out of her mouth, the sky lit up with a prolonged burst of fireworks.

Persistence, with the proper stagecraft, can do wonders for entrepreneurial romance.

On a more serious note, I cannot emphasize strongly enough how important it is for you, as an entrepreneur, to keep the faith and stay the course. I think of the twenty-six times I pitched the Rainforest Cafe to Lyle Berman without success and then got his support on my twenty-seventh try. What would have happened if I stopped at twenty-six?

Of course, there are some times when throwing in the towel

is not only the wisest course of action, but the only appropriate response. Nobody can afford to throw good money after bad forever; we all have physical, financial, and time limits. However, I do believe many entrepreneurs give up too easily; they walk away when things are not hopeless.

With Lyle, from the very beginning, I could tell he was interested in what I was doing, just not interested enough to commit to the project . . . yet. His response was the kind of reaction I call the "conditional no." It is a no but not a total no— an "I'm leaving the door open" kind of no. Those are the kinds of responses I'm looking for when I feel that persistence will prevail. As long as there's a sliver of interest in what I'm asking for (as when the chairman of the television agency in New York didn't give me an interview the first time around but told me to keep trying), then I'm going to keep pushing until I'm convinced that any further efforts will be futile.

Persist and prevail. The history books are full of famous, successful people that made their way to the winner's circle because they kept on trying: Trump, Disney, Walton, Hilton. They had pit-bull determination to reach their goals.

Do you know how many thousands of people went through our T-Rex restaurant concept in more than five years without making a deal? Nobody does R&D for five years. Nobody spends $14 to $15 million on a laboratory in a suburb of Minneapolis, filling warehouses with themed environments for restaurant and retail concepts. *Nobody*. It was a huge financial debt and a huge commitment of time and personnel. But we believed that it's impossible to put the time, money, energy, passion, and commitment into something and not have it work. We persisted until we succeeded.

Pit-bull determination isn't easy. As Newt Gingrich once observed, "Perseverance is the hard work you do after you get tired of doing the hard work you already did." I can relate to that. It's not easy persisting when that elusive goal is still not reached. But persist you must. The apple highest on the tree always leaves the sweetest taste.

CHAPTER 17

No Is Yes Waiting to Happen

"There are two ways to say yes: right away or after I change your mind."

—ANONYMOUS

Self-examination Question:
Are you the kind of person who will make a concentrated effort to convince somebody she might have made the wrong decision?

In a perfect world, the word *no* wouldn't exist. It wouldn't even be in the dictionary. Every request you made would be granted. It would be like that smiling loan manager at the car dealership with the sign on his desk: "We love to say yes."

But the entrepreneurial game isn't a perfect world. In fact, I strongly suspect that the vast majority of entrepreneurs have to endure an ocean of nos before getting to the Island of Yes. That's the way it is when you're asking other people to do you favors or lend you money or approve your plan.

Because no is the contemporary entrepreneur's constant companion, one has to learn how to deal with it and what steps to take to change no to yes.

Reacting to No

Having the right attitude when it comes to hearing no is critical for the entrepreneur. It involves developing the correct reactions for coping with the word when rejection is cast in your direction:

1. *You can't be shocked or crushed when you hear the word* no *because you will hear it, no matter how good you are.* I always steel myself for a no whenever I make an offer or ask for something from a client, customer, or investor. That is because most people, even if they like what you're offering, aren't likely to run up, pat you on the shoulder, and heap lavish praise on your efforts. Why should they? It puts them at a disadvantage in the negotiating department when it comes time

to talk cold, hard cash. If you're buying a house, do you make your highest offer first? Unlikely. You point out problems; you might even feign disinterest. If you're selling a house, do you accept the first price tendered? Probably not. You might even act haughty and highly insulted. Coming to an agreement is a process of give and take, and no is part of that process on the way to yes.

2. *You should think of no as a "four-letter word"— something you hate to hear and are loathe to accept.* Frankly, what I detest most is someone saying I can't do something. It's almost like challenging me to a duel. I have a can-do attitude and a can't-do response is like throwing down the gauntlet at my feet.

3. *You can't get discouraged and give up when the* no *word is uttered.*

4. *You need to believe you can change no into yes with the proper aptitude and effort.*

5. *You need to have faith in yourself and what you are trying to accomplish.* After all, if you don't believe in what you're doing, who will?

The Second No and the Conditional No

Unless things seem utterly hopeless, I always try to give a potential investor, client, or customer at least one chance to change his mind from no to yes. If that person says no a second time, I ask myself this critical question: *Was the no an emphatic no?* In other words, was it a solid rejection?

If the answer is yes, then I will probably look elsewhere (to another investor or client) for a favorable response. However, if the no was not *emphatic*, but rather a *conditional no*, then I will keep trying until I sense the no has become emphatic. This is where your good judgment and experience plays a major role in determining whether you persist or desist in dealing with an individual. Obviously, (a) the greater your belief in what you're selling, (b) the more important you perceive the person you are trying to convince to be, and (c) the greater your sense that the no is conditional and not emphatic, the longer and harder you should work to change no into yes and achieve an affirmative response to what you're proposing.

Turning No to Yes

I make it a habit to handle a first rejection from a potential investor differently than a second rejection. The first time I get a no, I usually try to sweeten the offer or take some action that will lead to a yes the second time around. After all, as mentioned previously, most people don't start out saying yes the first time around; they need a little prodding and some negotiating room.

Early in my career, when I was selling Proctor & Gamble ad spots to television stations in Chicago, I approached one account executive who represented several stations and made an offer she promptly refused. Of course, I was disappointed, but I wasn't ready to give up, either. I knew that a first no is only a final no if you stop asking. In this case, I got to be friends with the woman and discovered we shared something in common: we both wanted to try skydiving, but hadn't done it. And so I arranged for a one-day skydiving course where we learned the ins and outs of skydiving during an all morning lesson and then went for our actual skydive in the afternoon.

I remember the moment like it was yesterday. We were up at 3,500 feet and the executive had agreed to jump first. As she was making final preparations for her big moment, I handed her a contract for ad time and said, "Just in case something happens, would you like to do something really nice before you jump?" She didn't sign, but at least she was smiling as she left the aircraft.

It was a long way down. Fortunately, we both enjoyed the jump, suffered no noticeable bruises, and a few weeks later she did sign the agreement.

The moral of the story? Sometimes you have to be prepared to go the extra mile (or jump the extra 3,500 feet, as the case may be) to get a no changed to yes.

Because of my personality and extraverted nature, I will often do crazy things to swing a no to a yes. When I was still selling television advertising in Chicago, for example, I dealt with a buyer who wouldn't see me and wouldn't even speak with me on the phone. When I found out that she worked in a windowed office on the sixth floor of a nearby building, I tried a more persuasive way to introduce myself: I rented a crane and had myself hoisted to a position right outside her window. When I rapped on the window, she looked up and saw me suspended sixty feet off the ground, holding a sign that read, "I'm Steve Schussler. Can I make an appointment to see you?"

That got me into her office the very next day. She said she

thought what I did was funny and decided to see me because (and I am quoting her directly) "who knows what you'd do next had I said no." She made time for me and I wound up with a deal. What's more, my antics caused a big buzz in the industry, which helped me get more business.

There was also the time I was trying to sell ad time to the man who was vice president of marketing for The Coca-Cola Company. His name was Tom, and I could never get past his secretary to make my offer. I decided to get his attention, and hopefully some face time, by buying him a birthday cake and topping it off with candles I had purchased from a magic store— the kind that you can't blow out.

Cake in hand, I walked into the outer office where Tom worked and told the receptionist it was his birthday and I had this cake to deliver to him. "Oh, my gosh," the receptionist gasped in surprise, likely mortified she hadn't known. "He's giving a speech right now in the auditorium. Would you like to present the cake to him there?"

I agreed, not realizing there were five hundred people sitting in the room.

Of course, no one except Tom and I knew that it wasn't really his birthday when I walked in and everyone started singing "Happy Birthday." When I got on stage to give him the cake he had some very choice words for me, including, but not limited to swear words and death threats. He also asked who the hell I was. I told him and said I wanted to get his attention. Things got worse when he tried to blow out the trick candles and couldn't. But I ended up getting the order from him.

Of course, you can get in a lot of trouble pulling the kind of stunts I came up with to turn no into yes. It's all about timing, knowing how far you can or can't go with someone, and a bit of luck, too. In the case of Tom, I had heard he was a good sport, and fortunately my intel was good; otherwise his non-birthday might have been my last birthday.

The point of these examples is not to turn you into a major prankster or even a minor trickster. Instead, they're meant to encourage you to find an approach that fits your aptitude and personality to get people to change from no to yes. The very bold approaches I used in these examples fit my personality at that time in my life and was geared to work with people whom I felt would appreciate that particular style of persistence. I believe it worked not just because it got attention, but because once people saw what I was willing to do to land the account they started thinking, "Gee, if this is what he'll do just to get the account, think of what he'll be capable of doing once he has it."

Again, doing humorous, outlandish, or crazy things to sell yourself or your ideas is certainly not the only, or preferred, approach for getting someone to go from no to yes. I used some of my own examples simply to demonstrate that using the right attitude and your particular skills can go a long way in changing a negative response to a positive outcome.

CHAPTER 18

Learn from Failure; Graduate to Success

"The gem cannot be polished without friction; nor man perfected without trials."

—CHINESE PROVERB

Self-examination Question:
Can you experience failure and still retain the self-confidence necessary to seek success?

"Show me an entrepreneur who has never experienced failure and I'll show you a liar."

One of my early business partners made that claim more than thirty years ago. While there could be some exceptions to his rule, I doubt there are many. The very nature of the entrepreneurial life makes for a greater likelihood of failure. This is because true entrepreneurs are taking risks, trying new things, going places where no one else has ever been—and that entails the opportunity for great rewards, but also the very real possibility of disappointment and failure.

Many entrepreneurs have experienced the highs and lows, the ups and downs, the successes and failures that come with the entrepreneurial territory. I should know; I've taken a few major tumbles myself on the way to success. I'm here to tell you it can happen—that you can fail and still, like the fabled phoenix, rise from your own ashes and fly high once again. And I'm also here to tell you how you can do it. You do it through persistence: dogged, tenacious, determined persistence. Persistence is an entrepreneur's greatest ally for, as Ralph Waldo Emerson so aptly noted, "Our greatest glory is not in never failing, but in rising up every time we fail." When it comes to entrepreneurship, the real problem isn't failure—it's learning how to deal with it and using that information to graduate to success.

The first thing the entrepreneur must learn from failure is that it need not be permanent. The entrepreneur who lacks the capacity to bounce back and move beyond his difficulties is doomed never to taste success. It is important to learn from failure but not to wallow in it. Failure should act as a stimulus, not a paralysis.

The second thing the entrepreneur must learn from failure is humility. You need to be humbled by your mistakes, not crippled by them. Pride does truly goeth before the fall, and entrepreneurs must always be conscious of keeping their egos in check.

The third and final thing an entrepreneur must learn from failure is to appreciate success—both how precious it is to achieve and how difficult it is to maintain. In my office, I have what I call my "Wall of Fame and Wall of Shame." It's there to remind me that the higher you go the farther you can fall; it helps me celebrate my success but also keeps me mindful of my failures.

I would be less than honest if I told you I never had doubts about becoming a successful entrepreneur. I endured failures that made me wonder if I'd ever make it. There was the time when my Juke Box Saturday Night club in Minneapolis was failing, and my friends were abandoning me in droves. Then there were the years I couldn't find an investor for my Rainforest Cafe concept and I didn't have enough money to pay the gas bill. There were even the moments when people said I was crazy to pursue my dreams and I'd look in the mirror and wonder if they were right. These were bad times, really bad times. I was physically and psychologically decimated. I was financially crushed.

But I persisted and prevailed. I turned the corner and walked down a new street. It wasn't easy street, but it was paved with promise and headed in the direction I wanted to go. Good things happened; success grew out of failure, the phoenix flew. But the Wall of Fame and the Wall of Shame is always there to remind me of the thin line between joy and despair, prosperity and poverty, triumph and defeat. It keeps me in the proper balance between hubris and humility, self-aggrandizement and self-deprecation. It teaches me that failure is a place I don't want to be, underscores how easy it is to make a return visit, and reminds me that perseverance is the bedrock upon which success is built.

CHAPTER 19

Be Upbeat or Be Beat Down

*"Who cares if my glass is half empty or half full;
I still have something left to drink."*

—ANONYMOUS

Self-examination Question:
Can you remain generally optimistic
even when things are not going
your way?

I have a motto: "I've never had a bad day."

The first time my motto got quoted in the press was on the weekend the utility workers dug a twenty-five-foot hole in the street to cut off the gas to my house. A reporter came up to me and asked how I felt. Well, I wasn't feeling exactly jovial, but I was alive and the Earth was still circling the sun. "This is a setback," I admitted. "I need to get the gas back on."

"This has got to be the worst day of your life," the reporter surmised, obviously fishing for some juicy emotional response that would read well in the morning news.

"I've never had a bad day in my life," I responded flatly. And I meant it.

I guess that's always been my philosophy: learn to deal with adversity and move on. I consider myself to be lucky. Sure, I've had some rough times: I've been hit hard and been down, but at least I've been able to pick myself up. I can put up with the gas company and a lot worse. And you can, too!

If you want to be an entrepreneur, you have to maintain an upbeat attitude in the face of disappointment and loss. You need to keep the proper perspective. When things get difficult, guess what? It comes with the territory. You're fortunate to be an entrepreneur. You get to do your own thing and be your own boss. If it comes with certain costs, like suffering through some rough times, try to think like I do: proclaim there have been cloudy days, rainy days, tornado and hurricane days . . . *but never a bad day.*

Believe me, there have been some days that have tried my patience and tempted me to renounce my motto. One of those days involved a showing of my Rainforest Cafe concept. An important investor was scheduled to take the tour and I had rented a baboon to greet him at the front door and walk him inside. The baboon was dressed up and in the car on the way to my house when, about a mile away, it ripped its clothes off and smeared its excrement all over everything.

I learned that day it is a Guinness-level feat to sanitize a baboon covered in excrement, dress it, and bring its body odor to an acceptable level—all in ten minutes while working out of a gas station restroom in the dead of winter. The baboon went on with the show, but after that experience we always had an ample supply of baboon diapers on hand. Just to be on the safe side.

Then there was Easter Sunday 1995. At three o'clock in the morning, I got a call from security at the Mall of America informing me that our main three-thousand-gallon fish tank at the Rainforest Cafe had exploded. (Thank the Lord it hadn't happened at three o'clock in the afternoon when the restaurant was open. Who knows how many injuries would have occurred?) We had a few short hours to clean up the monumental mess, but we got it done and were open for business on schedule at 11 a.m. . . . with no one realizing what had happened. We put a large wrapper around the broken tank with a sign saying the fish were on vacation and we were making an exhibit that was bigger and better for customers to enjoy. We turned a potential disaster into a public relations coup. What could have been viewed as a disaster was now seen as something positive, a construction project to enhance the customer's dining experience at the restaurant.

I also recall moments when my financial resources were running on empty. One time I was walking to a meeting with my accountant and close friend, Tim Myslajek. Along the way there was a restaurant with an ornate wishing well situated near the front door. I stopped to dig out some coins from my pocket to make a wish. I couldn't find a single penny to toss into the well. That's how broke I was. I was totally out of money. Tim looked at me sadly and said, "This is a *really* bad day for you."

And I replied, "There's no such thing as a bad day."

You have a choice: be upbeat or be beat down. And remember that the best way never to have a bad day (at least where business and finances are concerned) is to convince yourself you won't.

Walt Disney once said, "All our dreams can come true—if we have the courage to pursue them." So have faith in yourself. Be a person of courage. Stand erect and move forward into the storm; the winds will subside and the sun will shine. Keep your eye on your dream and stay a steady course. Let your persistence, your pit-bull determination, see you through to your goal. As you move forward, be guided by the words of Winston Churchill: "Never, never, never, never give up."

SECTION IV

PEOPLE

CHAPTER 20

Have a Caring Attitude Toward All Living Things

"I will pay more for the ability to deal with people than any other ability under the sun."
—JOHN D. ROCKEFELLER

Self-examination Question:
Do you care about the feelings and needs of others and take active steps to help them achieve their personal goals?

Think back for a moment and identify someone you really respect—somebody for whom, if he asked you to go to the ends of the Earth, you would make the trip. Chances are this somebody is a person who cared about you. Giving others the sense you care about them is one of the most important elements when it comes to making a positive impression on them.

When it comes to making friends, influencing people, and being a good parent, spouse, or business partner, one of the most critical things you can do is care for those around you. People respond positively when they believe you care about them; they want to be around you, to be your friend, to do business with you. A willingness to care for others—and to *show* that caring attitude—is so important that I still carry around a quote from a book I read a long time ago. It says, simply, "If you care, you are there."

I am not speaking of false caring, or a situation where a person pretends to care about you so she can get something from you. An individual might be able to bluff for a while, but, in any meaningful, long-term relationship, such manipulative, insincere behavior will be discovered—and the consequences won't be pretty. Nor should they be. Caring is something that should flow honestly from the heart, from a true sense of concern for others, not from the head, where one puts forth a robotic, intellectual effort to feign caring in search of personal gain.

True caring for people should come naturally; it shouldn't be faked or forced. Some of my associates are amazed when I do things like send flowers in remembrance of a business associate's parents or fly cross-country to attend a friend's wedding. They think it's over the top. Perhaps for them it is, but it is my way of expressing my care for people and it's something I enjoy doing.

I know of a very successful businessman who has a sign on his office desk. It says, "What you think of me is none of my business." I can understand this thinking; it is usually undertaken by reserved, private individuals who feel it is intrusive to discover what other people feel about them. They focus on the trade, not the trader; the business deal, not the person making it.

I don't feel this way at all. What you think of me is very much my business. In fact, my business depends on it. That's because I can't effectively do business with people who don't care about me, and, conversely, I can build a much more effective business relationship with people who do. As an example, I remember when officials from Kansas City first approached me about putting our first T-Rex restaurant in their town. Initially, I wasn't very excited at the prospect. But when I met with the contingent of Kansas City officials and saw how much they cared about me and T-Rex, it made a real difference. I *wanted* to work with them and make a deal, which is exactly what happened.

If I sense that a customer or investor doesn't seem to care about me, it disturbs me and I want to know why. I'll ask questions or do what's necessary to discover where the problem lies. I do this because I want to correct the behavior that is causing the problem—not because I want the person's business (although I might), but because I care about people and I am unhappy if someone is disturbed by something I'm doing.

Now, obviously, you can't satisfy everybody and, because of basic human nature, there will always be some people who don't think much of you, no matter how effectively you care for them. If you can find no reasonable explanation for their behavior, chalk it up to chemistry or some other esoteric factor that makes certain people incompatible and move on. If you truly care for people, there will always be more people who will be happy to work with you than those who won't.

I do nice things for others because I want to—not to manipulate people or get something from them. If you care for the right reasons, you will probably get these things anyway, since one of the collateral benefits of caring for others is that they will want to do things in return . . . and that translates into a higher probability that they will buy into your entrepreneurial visions and support you in your efforts to succeed. In the next few chapters, I'll present some tried-and-true ways to care effectively for people.

CHAPTER 21

Make People Feel Special

"Pretend that every single person you meet has a sign around his or her neck that says, 'Make Me Feel Important.' Not only will you succeed in sales, you will succeed in life."

—MARY KAY ASH

Self-examination Question:
When was the last time you did something specifically to make somebody feel special?

Think about times in your life you've been singled out by somebody who made you feel special. Maybe this person praised you, or gave you an unexpected gift, or took the time to write a letter on your behalf. How did you feel toward this person? You may use any of a whole range of adjectives, and I suspect all of them would be positive. People want to feel special; it's a normal human desire, and I have yet to meet an individual who doesn't appreciate this kind of attention.

I know some entrepreneurs who practice this principle at the most rudimentary level. They send out a yearly birthday card to venture capitalists and other individuals they see as relevant to their business success. They might also send out holiday greeting cards and/or congratulatory notes for significant events such as anniversaries. In a sense, the person receiving this card might feel special; on the other hand, because these events occur on a regular, annual basis, the impact value of these cards is limited. People realize that a computer can be programmed to automatically send out cards on a specific date each year, so the act doesn't take much thought or planning.

A more meaningful way to make people feel special is to recognize them or their loved ones for events that *don't* occur on a predictable, regular basis. For example, a graduation, a birth in the family, a marriage, a promotion, the receipt of an award, or membership into a special organization are all good opportunities to show you've paid special attention to what is happening in their lives. Taking the time to recognize these occasions and send out the appropriate card is what will really make someone feel special.

Another great way to make people feel special is to phone them and say hello or send a written greeting when *no* special reason is involved. The call or the card is a potent reminder that you're thinking of them, that you care about them, that they're someone special.

I make it a point to combine all these approaches in dealing with my friends and business associates. I send out cards and I make calls, sometimes on significant dates and sometimes on a random day of my choosing.

People also feel special when you treat them as unique individuals. You can show this by taking notice of their personal lives and interests. For example, before I meet with clients or potential investors I learn as much as I can about them. Are they married? Single? What about kids? Do they have special hobbies? Pets? I want to get to know them on a personal basis, and my interest is genuine. I think it's important when you meet with people to be able to know the names of their spouses, their kids . . . even their pets.

Back in the days of our Juke Box Saturday Night club and restaurant, when we were planning to open a venue in a new city, I would first move there for a month. I wanted to meet face-to-face with the mayor, the chamber of commerce, and other important people in the community because I wanted them to feel special and know we saw their community as unique. In fact, once we opened our restaurant/nightclub, I made it the duty of the club manager to read all the town's papers so he could be up on the local news. Even putting a "Congratulations Graduating Seniors" message on our sign out front was important; it showed that we were involved in the community and saw our customers as special people.

Knowing more about the people you are dealing with not only provides information you can use to make them feel special, but it also gives you insight on how to interact with them more successfully.

A case in point: when we were pitching our T-Rex restaurant to officials in Kansas City, I needed to meet with the mayor to get her approval. When I found out she had been a schoolteacher, I decided to focus my presentation on the part of the restaurant where the mayor and I had a shared interest: the interactive, educational aspects of the venture. I told the mayor how we used focus groups of children to develop a simulated fossil dig and dinosaur information kits as an interactive learning experience. The mayor appreciated this aspect of our restaurant and gave the project a glowing review when she reported back to her political associates in Kansas City. She was a big part of the reason we got a generous financial grant to open T-Rex in her city.

Knowing enough about your client, customer, or investor to discover topics or points of common interest can really make the individual feel special (we all enjoy the chance to talk with someone about something we like) and, thus, more likely to support the project or idea you're recommending.

People also feel special when they are on the receiving end of a kind gesture. If I find out that a friend or associate is having trouble, I'll pick up the phone and give that person a call. I just want to reassure him and let him know there are friends out there who care about him. Sometimes the person I call will want to vent. I listen. Sometimes I'm asked for advice. I'll give it if I think I'm qualified to respond. Usually what I get from these calls is appreciation for my concern—and a great feeling that I made a small but positive difference in somebody's life.

Building friendships with people also makes them feel special. J. C. Penney once claimed that "Every business is built on friendship." I'm not sure that's true in all cases, but I do believe that friendships help forge stronger business ties. In the case of the entrepreneur, the start of a friendship with a business contact can blossom into something very joyous: a great relationship and business partnership at the same time.

Finally, giving people praise is a great way to make them feel special. This approach is particularly useful in a work setting if you are managing people. Not all entrepreneurs will have a staff to oversee, but if you do, a little praise can go a long way in creating goodwill and motivating team members in your organization.

Complimenting an employee for a job well done is probably the simplest and most basic way to make her feel special in the workplace. Management professor and author Dr. Michael LeBoeuf sums it up this way: "There are two things people want more than sex and money . . . recognition and praise."

When this praise is given publicly, it can be even more powerful and make people feel even more special. I compliment my work associates and team members whenever I get a chance. Whether you are offering team members extra pay or verbal praise, the important thing is to let your team members know you appreciate their time, effort, and accomplishments.

I am blessed with a tremendous team of dedicated men and women who are a large part of the reason we have been successful in our business ventures. I do what I can to make them feel special . . . because they are! When one of my teammates stays late to complete a project or works extra hard to give me his best effort, I make it a point to tell him how much I appreciate his dedication. Sometimes I have the chance to do this in a public forum. Recently, I gave a speech to a group of Minnesota businesspeople and took the opportunity to honor my teammates with special "silver stars" inscribed with their names and a brief message about how vital they are in my life. It's important to remind your team members that you think they're special. My hard-working staff deserves this, and so does yours.

CHAPTER 22

Help Others Achieve Their Goals

"Successful people are always looking for opportunities to help others. Unsuccessful people are always asking, 'What's in it for me?'"

—BRIAN TRACY

Self-examination Question:
Are you willing to help other people succeed even when it's not a requirement of your job to be of assistance?

In my entrepreneurial career, I have gained great benefits—both in terms of personal satisfaction and professional advancement—by helping other people reach their objectives. You don't have to believe in karma to follow this recommendation, but, if what comes around truly does go around, then following my suggestion certainly can't hurt.

Let me give you a few examples. Many years ago, a woman attended a workshop where I gave a speech on the joys of being an entrepreneur. At the time, she had been thinking of buying a business; after my presentation, she decided to go the entrepreneurial route and develop a business of her own. Her name was Maxine Clark, and, as you might remember from an earlier chapter, she founded Build-A-Bear, a fantastically successful enterprise. How did this help me? It was Maxine whom I approached to form a strategic partnership. We agreed to take advantage of her established Build-A-Bear product and experience, while she would get a new retail product, Build-A-Dino, to produce further revenue for her company. Coincidence? Certainly. But it's interesting that, as I helped Maxine achieve her goals, she turned around and helped me achieve mine. Build-A-Dino is one of our top-selling items.

Then there's the story of Maribeth Bisienere. She is a senior executive at Disney who assesses different projects and helps determine if they are suitable for placement in any of the theme parks. At one point in our relationship, she asked if I would give a lecture on leadership to some of the Disney team members. I couldn't be there on the date she needed, so I made a video of myself speaking on the topic and sent it to her to use. Then, about a year later, I was with her on a business trip to visit Disney's Paris operation when she met with a French gentleman who owned a tethered balloon company and was looking to undertake some joint ventures. I was interested in the man's business and we began coming up with new ideas. There was nothing in it for me; I just thought I could be of some help and I enjoyed sharing my knowledge and experience with him.

Later on, I found out that my behavior with Maribeth—the time I took to make the video and to help out her French business contact—made a big impact on her. She told me that, "Because of your willingness to share and help others, I'm much more apt to do business with you." I didn't do either of these things for personal gain, nor did I expect any. Yet the pleasure I received assisting others had a collateral benefit: it helped me make a better impression on a person who saw me as a more viable business partner because of it.

CHAPTER 23

Managing Perception for Maximum Impact

"All the world's a stage; how do you wish to be seen by your audience?"

—ENGLISH AUTHOR, UNKNOWN

Self-examination Question:

Do you ever purposely behave in a specific manner to influence how another person will perceive you?

I've written a word just below this sentence. Take a moment, if you would, and read the word aloud:

Unionized

What did you think of? If you are like most people, you read the word in a way that describes a business organization where workers are represented by a union. One would say the company is "unionized." That is because the majority of us spend most of our time working with people and dealing with organizations where unions are part of the business landscape. However, what if you were a biochemist? Then you might read the word in a different way: *un-ionized.* Why? Because ions are more common than labor unions in your line of work and your frame of reference, and we know people perceive the world differently based on their experiences and beliefs.

In the world of interpersonal relationships, you can use what social scientists refer to as "perception management" to influence the way people perceive you. Perception management involves acting in certain ways to create in others a specific impression of you—hopefully, a positive impression. If you use it effectively, you can head off a lot of serious problems and interpersonal conflicts.

For example, when we first opened our Rainforest Cafe, PETA decided to protest the restaurant's use of live parrots. Organization members were quite vocal about their feelings and even threw what appeared to be blood at some of our restaurant staff. We were angry and hurt. No one loves animals and birds more than I do, particularly parrots; I've had them as pets since I was a teenager. The question was, what should we do about the protests?

We decided to use perception management. Several of us joined PETA, and, the next time the protesters gathered in front of the restaurant, we went outside, showed them our PETA membership cards, and indicated we were one of them. We explained to the protesters that our birds were not taken from the wild. They were hand-raised, domestically fed babies. We loved our birds—and what was wrong with that?

The PETA protesters went away.

Another time, I faced a different kind of crisis. We had decided to hold a major fundraiser for some political candidates at my Jukebox Saturday Night club and restaurant. At that time, there was an up-and-coming union that was involved in trying to organize restaurants and hotels in Minnesota. The organization decided to make a statement by trying to unionize my team. The union knew that politicians normally respect picket lines, so union members decided to throw pickets around my place and stop the political candidates from entering my establishment. They actually had a guy dressed in a huge, furry rat uniform standing near our front door with a picket sign in his hand. He was probably the only comfortable person on the picket line; it was a bitterly cold, windy Twin Cities winter evening.

I decided to try a little perception management. The people on that picket line had a very negative opinion of us, so I asked my team to make some hot cocoa and chocolate chip cookies and bring the items out to the protesters, who drank the cocoa, ate the cookies . . . and left! What was supposed to be a five-hour protest lasted fifteen minutes. Our goodwill gesture helped alter the pickets' perception of us as "bad guys" and helped create a behavioral outcome that we dearly wanted. It also got us good press; people who observed the situation were so impressed that our goodwill gesture had defused the situation that it was reported in the paper the next day.

Sometimes it is important to use perception management to create the appropriate image or belief you want a person or group of people to have about you and/or your creations. Because I wanted people to see Juke Box Saturday Night as a wholesome, clean, fun place to party, rather than a tough joint with hard drinking and barroom brawls, I used perception management to underscore this atmosphere. We used words to create the appropriate environment. For example, we didn't have "bouncers"; we employed "doormen." Bouncers are big, muscular, and ugly, while our doormen were neatly dressed and welcomed guests to the club in a friendly, conversational manner. I also employed a "master of ceremonies" instead of a "disc-jockey." Our master of ceremonies did more than spin records. He knew how to communicate with both an eighty-five-year-old grandmother and a twenty-two-year-old college kid.

Perception management is about getting people to see you and what you do in a positive light. What you don't want to do is say things and/or act in a manner that will create negative impressions and the unwanted consequences that are certain to follow. I learned this lesson as a teenager, back when I was running the poker game at the Silver Gull Beach Club. There I was, pocketing hundreds of dollars a weekend with no problems until I started bragging about my good fortune. By opening my big mouth, I shot myself in the foot. People get jealous, and jealous people will do their best to bring down the object of their jealousy, which, in this case, was me. If I had remained silent and just gone about my business, I might have kept my summer windfall going for another five years. As it was, my bragging cost me a dream job.

Shooting off my mouth was a failure of perception management. It violated a cardinal rule: when you're doing well, keep quiet and don't reveal the degree of your success to others. Be particularly careful not to boast or brag about how much money you make. Never forget that jealousy is everywhere and that, when it comes to money, people are definitely concerned and jealous over how much other people make. You can say all day long that people don't care about how much money a person makes, but it just isn't true. People *do* care, and they care enough to sabotage individuals who flaunt their riches or shove their good fortune in other people's faces.

A friend once told me, "Get rich in the dark." I never quite understood what he meant until I experienced my summer job debacle. Now I understand it fully and live by his dictum as best I can.

As a final example of perception management, let me describe a conflict that arose over the appropriate start time for our T-Rex Grand Opening at Disney World. We had planned to have the party from 2 to 4 p.m. Then, Disney called and suggested an earlier time frame—11 a.m. to 1 p.m.—to make it easier for reporters to get coverage ready for the evening news. We thought about it a long time and decided that an eleven o'clock opening was not celebratory or special; it was lunch hour. The afternoon time slot made the ribbon-cutting ceremony something special. It came down to the difference between perceiving the opening ceremony as "lunch" or a "reception" and we opted for the latter.

Image is important when you're trying to create the appropriate mind-set. Perception management is a way you, as an entrepreneur, can shape your image to fit the way you want to be perceived by others.

CHAPTER 24

Create Positive Press

Self-examination Question:
Do you make a concerted effort
to establish good media contacts
and use them to generate positive
publicity for the work that you do?

Some entrepreneurs seem to have a love-hate relationship with the press. This is unfortunate. Getting media attention—*positive* attention—is critical for a large number of entrepreneurs. In fact, publicity might well be seen as the lifeblood of their creations. Without it, the creations die.

I actively seek media attention in my business operations. In fact, when dealing with reporters and other members of the media, I have a "two-hour" rule: I personally return all media calls within two hours of the time I receive them. I've learned to respect other people's time and I know that many reporters are working against deadlines. It's not only common courtesy that makes me follow my two-hour rule; it's also the realization that the faster I call back, the better the chance a story about my work will be written or aired or that my involvement in a particular story will be included.

I also answer my own phone. Members of the media are often shocked by this, since they expect to run a gauntlet of subordinates before reaching me. I've found that they appreciate this personal touch—a sentiment often reflected in their willingness to give me more of their time and coverage in the stories they file. When speaking with the media, I always try to give reporters and newscasters everything they ask for—and more. I'm always looking for additional angles or news I can feed them that might whet their appetites for extra information on what I'm doing. Many is the time that a reporter started out asking me a question that was to be a small part of a story and, by the end of the conversation, my project or commentary had become the major focus of the article. As I said in an earlier chapter, you're not only selling your product, you're selling yourself, too.

Reporters are people looking to do a good job. If you can help them by providing information and, at the same time, exude enthusiasm, it's going to make a positive difference in the way you're portrayed in the media. "PR" is an abbreviation for "Public Relations," but it could also stand for "Personal Relationships." More than similar initials connect these two terms. The personal relationship you establish with the media will influence the quality of public relations you receive.

Knowing the right people can also generate good press for you and your business. Don't shy away from meeting and building relationships with people of importance. Networking with well-known personalities is not only critical for expanding your base of operations, but it also builds face recognition and generates good opportunities for publicity. Getting to know important people can sometimes occur by accident, such as when you meet somebody of significance sitting next to you on a cross-country flight, so take advantage of such chance encounters to build new relationships. Other times it can happen as the result of actions you take to help people of importance reach their objectives. Because I am active in political fund-raising, for example, I have had the privilege of getting to know and become friends with several nationally elected officials.

One great way to generate good press for your product or your company is often overlooked by otherwise savvy entrepreneurs: your telephone answering system. I have always believed that your first contact with a potential customer, investor, or client is critically important and, often, that first contact is by phone. Therefore, what the caller hears when your phone is answered is crucial and can go a long way to encourage or discourage further interest in you or what you have to offer.

If you can afford it, I think it is wise to invest in a human operator, so that the first thing a caller hears when dialing up your business is another person, *not* a machine. Moreover, whether your phone system employs a person or a machine, it is important that the call be answered in a timely fashion. Waiting more than five rings to hear a response turns a caller off. Further, a caller should not be placed on hold for more than a minute. (If hold times are longer than a minute, one way to reduce the chance of losing callers is to provide a "countdown system" where the caller is informed how long his expected wait time will be. It is important that the wait time experienced does not exceed the wait time promised.)

That hold time provides an opportunity that is often overlooked: the chance to give a captive audience a great sales pitch. Canned music or dead silence during wait times is ridiculous. Give yourself some good press right there on the telephone. Maybe you can even sell the caller before you ever pick up the phone!

Web sites can also generate positive press. A good Web site should favorably reflect you and your company's ideas, products, and/or services. It should be easily navigated and provide visitors with obvious ways to contact you and/or your company. An attractive, well-organized, useful Web site is one of the great advertising tools in the entrepreneur's arsenal. Use it. In addition, reporters and other members of the media will often decide whether or not to interview you based on the impressions they get from your Web site. Make those impressions positive ones.

Here is one final suggestion for generating good press: throw a party! I guess this is a predictable recommendation coming, as it does, from a themed restaurant owner, but—really—doing a good job of hosting people at a social function is a great way to get positive exposure and press at the same time. When I throw a party, I want it to be special because that is the message I want to send to my guests: *you are special.* I ban "blah" birthday cakes at birthday parties. You know, the frosted layer cake or the sheet cake, your standard kind of dessert. What I want to give my guests is something different—maybe an ice-cream cake or something with chocolate waterfalls or do-it-yourself toppings. And it's important to remember the details at these kind of parties: If I'm serving finger foods, I want to make sure there are ample napkins and toothpicks in easy reach. If I'm offering beverages, I want to make sure there are plenty of clean glasses and ice to go around. There should also be enough places for guests to deposit their trash—or, better yet, enough catering staff to remove the trash before the guests have to deal with it.

One final note about parties: if you're invited to one that can affect your business, go. Even if you don't feel like it, or you're an introvert, or you have a heavy appointment schedule, it doesn't matter. Make time to drop by. You don't have to stay long. By showing up, your presence validates your host and strengthens your mutual relationship. Plus, there's always the chance for a little networking with other guests while making your appearance.

CHAPTER 25

The Power of Trust in Transactions

"If people like you they'll listen to you, but if they trust you they'll do business with you."

—Zig Ziglar

Self-examination Question:
Do you recognize the crucial role trust plays in successful business relationships and therefore do everything possible to establish and maintain trust between yourself and your clients?

I believe that trust is the bedrock upon which all meaningful human relationships are built, and I've learned that, in my business, an entrepreneur is no better than her word. Trust is critical to potential investors because, as I've noted before, they're buying you as well as what you have to offer. If they can't trust you, how can they invest in you?

William Shakespeare wrote, "No legacy is so rich as honesty." Just as trust is the foundation for all meaningful relationships, honesty is the basis for trust. If you have conducted your affairs in an honest manner, you will always be able to look your investors in the eye (and yourself in the mirror), even if your venture fails. Further, if you do fail, but you do so with honesty intact, you are more likely to find new investors, or retain old ones who are willing to take another chance on you. People can risk taking a second chance because they can trust what you say. Who would want to invest money in a person who can't be trusted to tell the truth?

Honesty played a critical role in one of the most important business deals I ever made. In the 1990s, I was invited to appear before a group of Disney executives to discuss the possibility of placing a Rainforest Cafe in one of the company's theme parks. Disney, obviously, is very concerned about its image, and that includes the people with whom the company does business. The term "squeaky-clean" comes to mind when trying to describe what Disney is looking for when it screens team members, vendors, and business partners.

On the day of my presentation, I was ushered into a large boardroom where several Disney executives were sitting around a conference table. Before I even had a chance to present my prepared statement, one of the executives asked me a question:

"How do you think Disney feels about gambling? Isn't Lyle Berman, chairman of your board [of Rainforest Cafe], involved in gaming?"

"Yes, he is," I answered. "And he does a great job and gives hundreds of Native Americans jobs."

The executive Mr. Dare considered my answer for a moment, looked at me intently, and offered up another question: "I understand you had a place called Juke Box Saturday Night and, for a while, you had topless dancing on the second floor. How do you think Disney feels about that?"

I remember thinking to myself at that point that Disney was a dead deal. I felt like I had just been kicked in the groin. Between Lyle's involvement with gaming and the issues of topless dancing at my nightclub, what chance did I have to get Disney on board with my project? I could feel myself begin to sweat profusely. I did the only thing I knew how to do: I answered his question with complete candor and honesty.

I fully disclosed what had happened at Juke Box Saturday Night. I explained how we had suffered a financial setback and owed money in taxes. I described how our nightclub and restaurant weren't doing well and how somebody had come to us and asked to rent out the second floor of our building for limited adult entertainment. I admitted I never should have done it, that I regretted my decision. I explained that we shut the operation down as quickly as we could. The people had a one-week lease and, when it was up, we didn't renew it. I took responsibility for my mistake, acknowledging that the problem had occurred on my watch and shouldering the full blame for it.

After I finished answering the question, I began my formal

presentation. I did the best I could under the circumstances, but I was worried it wouldn't be enough.

When I finally heard the news that Disney had given us the green light to go ahead with the restaurant plans, I was both surprised and pleased. Of course I was glad to have the deal, but I was still a bit in shock that I'd pulled it off.

A few years later, I had a chance to speak with that executive about Disney's decision and what had happened that day back in the conference room. I learned that the Disney executives knew everything about me ahead of time, including the adult entertainment snafu at my Juke Box restaurant. If I hadn't been totally honest with them and expressed my remorse over what had happened at my club, the executive told me candidly, the deal probably would have never gone through.

Honesty truly is the best policy. Truth is the gateway to trust. An honest, trustworthy entrepreneur is not always the easiest person to be, particularly in trying times, but is the kind of person, I believe, we should all strive to become.

CHAPTER 26

Don't Burn Bridges (Just Cross Them Carefully the Second Time Around)

"Never cut what you can untie."

—JOSEPH JOUBERT

Self-examination Question:
Are you willing to give a person a second chance?

At some point in your entrepreneurial life (maybe at many points) somebody is going to disappoint you or, possibly, take advantage of you. When this happens, should you just write this person off and decide never to work with him again? There's a real temptation to say yes and be done with this type of individual for good. Why not? The person has either let you down or screwed you up. To hell with him!

But wait a moment. People change. Times change. Conditions change. Individuals who hurt you in the past might be able to help you in the future, so I wouldn't be so quick to dismiss them out of hand. I'd just be a lot more cautious in dealing with them the second time around.

Some of my biggest opportunities and successful ventures have involved people who, earlier in my life, had caused me disappointment and/or problems. Take, for example, my own father, Jules. He left home when I was young, pretty much abandoning our family, and, for a long time, we were estranged. Yet, he is the person responsible for getting me together with Lyle Berman, the venture capitalist who would eventually give me the investment money I needed to make my Rainforest Cafe dream a reality.

How did my dad do it? With a lot of nerve and chutzpah.

He was working out in Las Vegas at the time and had gone to watch the World Series of Poker. While he was there, he noticed that one of the players was Lyle, whom he recognized as a venture capitalist from Minnesota. When play was halted for a fifteen-minute bathroom break, my father actually snuck by security and sat down in Lyle's chair, right in front of $350,000 in chips. When Lyle returned, he was in for a shock: my father was sitting in his chair as if he was ready to play the next hand of poker. Once he got over his initial surprise, Lyle asked my dad to get up and leave.

"Sir," said my dad, looking Lyle in the eye, "I'm not going until you agree to meet my son who lives in Minneapolis."

At that point, Lyle started to call for a security guard to throw my dad out. But he stopped when my dad pulled a $50 bill from his pocket and said, "Here, this is for you. You've *got* to meet my son. He's got a great concept for a restaurant you have to see to believe."

At that point, Lyle realized where my dad was coming from. He was accustomed to people pitching him ideas, just not from his chair at the World Series of Poker. So he gave my father his $50 back and handed him a business card. "Have your son call my assistant and set up an appointment," he said, "and please get out of my seat."

My dad went directly home and called me at three o'clock in the morning, described what he had done, and told me to schedule an appointment. I did as he said and, as the TV newscasters are fond of saying, "the rest is history."

Crazy, isn't it? My dad, who had been one of my biggest disappointments in his role as a father, came through for me much later in his life. After what happened in my childhood, I could have permanently burned the bridge between us, but I didn't—and my dad did better the second time around, when I was an adult. I'm glad to say we reconciled and shared some good times together before he died a few years ago.

There have been other times when my commitment not to burn bridges has proven beneficial. My most dramatic business example involves Landry's, the restaurant chain that purchased Rainforest Cafe at a fire-sale price. I was unhappy with the sale

when it happened. I thought we could have done better and tried
to raise capital to take the company public. I got together with
David Siegel (the largest time-share owner in the world), Herb
and Mel Simon (at the time, owners of Mall of America), and
Robert Earl, owner of Planet Hollywood, to see if a deal could
be achieved, but we failed. In the end Landry's won out, and
I remember expressing my frustration to the top executive at
Landry's, Tilman Fertitta, who was instrumental in making the
purchase. To make matters worse, not only did Tilman win the
financial battle, but he made changes to the restaurant that were
antithetical to my beliefs about what I thought the restaurant
should be and what it should represent.

From my vantage point, Tilman Fertitta, who is as
passionate about his business as I am about my creations, had
changed my vision at Rainforest Cafe. To make matters worse,
he proclaimed that the acquisition of Rainforest Cafe was one
of his greatest business decisions—and was quick to mention
how he had purchased the properties at such a great price. Talk
about rubbing salt in the wound! And, to top it off, once he
had control of Rainforest, he re-engineered the menu, including
our signature, world-famous lobster pasta dish by changing the
bowtie pasta that was an integral part of the selection's appeal.
I decided that Tilman Fertitta was a brash, arrogant, bargain-
basement, bottom-feeding business acquisition nemesis.

One would suspect that, given what had transpired between
myself and Tilman, I'd never talk to him again, let alone work
with him. But I did. In fact, I did so to the tune of a deal worth
$100 million involving our T-Rex and Yak & Yeti restaurants. I
still wasn't happy about his handling of the Rainforest restaurants,
but I came to understand that Tilman was a good restaurant

operator, that he could cut costs, expand outlets, improve the quality of the food and the consistency of the guest experience, and make a profit. I realized that I could disagree with some of his policies, but still appreciate him as an astute businessperson, and now we even agree on the change in bowtie pasta.

At the end of the day, what was significant about my relationship with Tilman was that we both came to respect each other. He respected me for my creative talents and I respected him as someone who could run complex businesses successfully and had the courage to invest in my concepts when significant financial risk was involved. He certainly wasn't a bottom-feeder when he shelled out multimillions to invest in my restaurants and, this time, this was no fire-sale. Tilman was a man who had the courage of his convictions to take a big chance on my ideas, and I owe him greatly for his faith in, and financial backing of, my projects.

Sometimes the desire to burn bridges has to do with ego issues. Don't fall victim to this danger. Many entrepreneurs have big egos that get in the way of good business decisions. It's not that I lack an ego; after all, I'm human, too. But I try to keep it in check when making deals. Sometimes price is more important than pride.

I recall one particularly acrimonious business meeting where some nasty comments were exchanged along with some really biting insults. Nobody was going to budge; everyone was angry. The two investors I was speaking with said they wanted nothing more to do with me; the deal was off. They told me to leave. I did, but not permanently. I went to the bathroom, took about ten minutes to let everyone cool off (including myself), and walked back into the room. I gave one of the partners a hug and told him we were going to get this deal done and I was sorry for some of the things I had said.

What I learned that day reconfirmed my belief that ego can be a killer, especially an unchecked ego. Most entrepreneurs need to have a healthy ego, but you also have to be realistic. That's a very delicate balance—the kind of balance you need to cross a bridge you tumbled off the first time around.

SECTION V

PHILANTHROPY

CHAPTER 27

Entrepreneurial Social Responsibility

"No one is useless in this world who lightens the burden of another."

—CHARLES DICKENS

Self-examination Question:
Do you try to incorporate sustainability and socially responsible practices in your business?

One day, early in my entrepreneurial career, I remember listening to Bob Hope, who said, "If you haven't got any charity in your heart, you have the worst kind of heart trouble." I thought a lot about that comment. It made me realize there is more to life than simply making money. Sure, I believe that getting is important—but so is giving back. Some of my pragmatic friends might argue with me and say that the only goal of the entrepreneur should be financial gain. I disagree. To these pragmatists I would say that helping others while helping yourself is not counterproductive. Quite the opposite, in fact—it can even be synergistic. Thus, the old adage: "You can't help someone uphill without getting closer to the top yourself."

I find that helping others is refreshment for my soul and gives me a sense of purpose that transcends dollars and makes real sense. In fact, some of my fondest entrepreneurial memories involve times I incorporated social responsibility into my business plan. There was the time, for instance, when we were building our first Rainforest Cafe at the Mall of America, that I decided to hire the homeless and give them jobs spraying fire retardant on the outside of artificial greenery (so it couldn't catch fire in the restaurant). My idea was to give them a chance to get off the streets and back on their feet. It was the kind of work where you didn't need to wear clean clothes or be immaculately groomed to get the work done.

I remember taking some of my staff and scouring areas under bridges and in abandoned buildings where the homeless congregated and provided our potential labor pool. The experience was humbling. When all was said and done, my attempt at social activism resulted in the good, the bad, and the ugly.

The "ugly" was the reality of what happens when you try to pull somebody off the streets. We were dealing with people who had drug and alcohol problems, some who stole, others who came in late or didn't show up at all. The "bad" was it cost us twice as much money to hire and train the homeless as it did our other workers. But the "good" involved the success stories: the homeless guys who left the streets and became productive, successful citizens.

One guy's name was Jim. He had been living on the street and in shelters before he worked with us. After his time with us, he ended up getting himself a steady job and his own apartment. He cut back on his drinking and reconnected with his family. Jim's story, and those like it, made all our efforts worthwhile. It cost our company money, but I'd do it again in a heartbeat.

Social responsibility is something that comes with the territory, particularly when your territory is an establishment that serves liquor.

Way back in the 1970s, when I was running Juke Box Saturday Night, we offered patrons who had too much to drink a free ride home. This was long before most bars and nightclubs were offering such a service. We didn't have to do this, but I felt it was the right thing to do.

There were several ways we ensured that our intoxicated patrons didn't drive home. One approach involved selecting a designated driver. (Our DD program was recognized by the U.S. Department of Transportation as one of the top five programs of its type in the country.) If a group of people came into the club together, and one of the members was willing to abstain from drinking alcoholic beverages, he was given a special pin. He was then served soft drinks on the house all night long so he could take his alcohol-consuming friends home safely. Another approach involved our doormen, who were trained to check out all patrons as they left the club. Our team members were required to complete an alcohol-awareness training course and, if they decided based on the evaluation techniques they'd learned that somebody was too drunk to drive, the club paid for that person to get a taxi ride home.

Probably our most successful and expensive approach to keeping our drunk patrons from getting behind the steering wheel of their cars was based on some research we had conducted at Juke Box. We discovered that people didn't like to give their car keys to a stranger and then take a taxi home. The problem was that they woke up the next morning wondering what happened to their cars. So we instituted a program where we persuaded the patrons who were too drunk to drive to let us tow their cars to their homes. We spent about $100,000 per year for two tow trucks, but it was worth it because it got us involved in the community and, most important, saved lives.

Our themed restaurants are also concerned with being socially responsible and encouraging respect for and conservation of the environment. In its early years, our Rainforest Cafes promoted a "rescue the rain forest" mentality. We contributed part of the restaurant's profits to environmental causes and sent our bird curators to the elementary and high schools in the area to teach children about the beauty of the rainforests and how they were endangered and needed protection. Emphasizing sustainability and being "green" in our themed attractions is very important to me, and I work hard with my team to keep environmental awareness in the forefront of our minds. It is something all businesses need to do and, hopefully, *will do* in the years to come.

CHAPTER 28

The Importance of Entrepreneurial Philanthropy

"We make a living by what we get; we make a life by what we give."

—Winston Churchill

Self-examination Question:
Do you believe it is important to "give back" some portion of your wealth to support charitable causes?

B ooker T. Washington said it perfectly: "If you want to lift yourself up, lift up someone else." I can think of no better way to do this than through philanthropy. I truly believe a greater award awaits the giver than the receiver when it comes to undertaking philanthropic activity. When you invest your time, energy, or money in serving others, you will gain great dividends in your own life.

A doctor friend once told me about a scientific study conducted in the United States. It showed that regular volunteer work dramatically increased life expectancy. Men who did no volunteer work were two-and-a-half times as likely to die during the study as men who volunteered once a week. I wasn't really sure I believed my friend until I read a book by Peter McWilliams entitled *You Can't Afford the Luxury of a Negative Thought*. According to the author, "Doing good for others enhances the immune system, lowers cholesterol, strengthens the heart, decreases chest pains, and reduces stress. A study at Harvard showed that even *thinking* about doing service produced positive psychological results." Maybe we should get involved in philanthropic activities as if our lives depended on it—they just might!

Do these findings come as a surprise? They shouldn't. Think of the times you have served others. Remember the good feelings you experienced? The joy of giving your time, service, or money to others is more than a noble calling, it is a pleasurable one. It is uplifting, a high without the need for drugs or alcohol. It is an affirmation of the human spirit . . . and the spirit within you soars. As the writer Eric Hoffer observed, "Kindness can become its own motive. We are made kind by being kind." And, as humanitarians have long pointed out, "A man's true wealth is the good he does in this world."

When it comes to my philanthropic work, I have a special charity I endorse and support. It was founded by an incredibly dedicated philanthropist, Kim Valentini, who gives amply of her time and inspiration to ensure its success. It is called Smile Network International and exists solely to help children from third-world countries who cannot afford medical services receive surgeries to repair cleft palates and lips *free of charge*. Every penny raised for this charity goes directly to the costs of performing these life-changing surgeries. For $500, our doctors and nurses can fix the cleft palate or cleft lip of a child and put a smile on her face forever.

In the United States, we take such surgical miracles for granted. But in third-world countries that just doesn't happen. And without surgical intervention the child's life will never be the same. I have personally witnessed how kids with these facial disfigurements are treated. They are stared at, ridiculed, shunned. Many don't attend school; they're kept locked up at home because their families are embarrassed to have them seen in public. It is a life no person would want to, or should have to, endure.

Surgically repairing a child's facial disfigurement changes his life forever. To see the change is truly a blessing. I've worked in the hospitals where these medical miracles are performed. I've held the kids before and after the operations. And I've been there when the kids smile for the first time and their parents cry for pure joy. It is the most heartwarming experience you can possibly imagine.

I am devoted to Smile Network because I believe in it with all my body and soul. I take a portion of the money I earn from all my entrepreneurial activities, including this book, and donate it to Smile Network. (Perhaps you might decide to contribute to this worthy cause as well. Information on the charity can be found at www.smilenetwork.org.)

Of course, in the final analysis, whether you contribute to my charity of choice is not the most important issue here. What's critical is that you contribute something to some charity, whatever that charity might be. What I'm trying to emphasize is that, as an entrepreneur, you have an opportunity (even an obligation) to give something back in proportion to what you have received—to be philanthropic as well as profitable.

It is a noble calling to share with the less fortunate a portion of what you have earned, a gift that shows your sense of caring for others. It is something we can all do to change the world for the better and, in the process, ourselves as well. For as Albert Pike so eloquently reminds us, "What we have done for ourselves alone dies with us; what we have done for others and the world remains and is immortal."

Some Final Thoughts

"No one can cheat you out of ultimate success but yourself."

—RALPH WALDO EMERSON

"Will you look back on life and say, 'I wish I had,' or 'I'm glad I did'?"

—ZIG ZIGLAR

No One Creates in a Vacuum

There are so many people to thank, so many stories, so much personal involvement by so many that sometimes it's overwhelming to remember all of those responsible for my success. I probably could write a book just about all of you and how you have influenced my life. The best thing I can do is to continue with all of the beautiful life lessons I've learned from interacting with you and try to contribute back what you have given me. This book is not complete without my heartfelt thanks to the following:

My mother, Gloria Palazzo, who from the time I was eight years old worked to support me along with my two brothers, Robert and John. With my mother divorced and single, we moved out of a prosperous neighborhood and rather large home where we all had our own bedroom (I even had a brass bed) to a very modest second-floor apartment where my brothers and I shared a room. How she was able to pay for everything, take care of us, clean, cook, and work with three boys and no child support is beyond comprehension. My mother worked managing a couple of gift shops in the Grand Canyon, and then learned Spanish and entered the Peace Corps, moving to Ecuador and working with the indigenous people. Now at seventy-seven years old, she is stunningly beautiful and living in Lake Chapala, Mexico, outside of Guadalajara, an accomplished artist still creating and experiencing life's adventures.

My dad, Jules Schussler, who died November 6, 2004, lived and retired in Las Vegas, Nevada. Dad tried very hard later in life to make up for the years of not seeing his family and not supporting my mother. He always enjoyed the action of craps and occasionally worked as an outspoken front man for a poker room in Las Vegas. Dad watched Lyle Berman play in the World Championship of Poker; he interrupted the game when it was announced that Lyle was from Minneapolis, and proceeded to pitch Lyle on meeting me. His 3 a.m. phone call to me, telling me to grab a pen and write Lyle's name and number down, began my roller-coaster ride. Lyle became my partner in Rainforest Cafe.

So my father was a salesman and my mother an artist—I guess I ended up with a little bit of both. I owe them gratitude for raising us the best they knew how. My brothers and I turned out great!

My childhood best friend, Eddie Silverman, and his family—Diane, Joanne, Betty, and Marty—who owned Island Lake Camp in Starrucca, Pennsylvania, where I worked waiting tables and taught waterskiing to defray the cost of going to camp. I cannot tell you what amazing lessons you learn early in life living outside your own home.

My uncle, Ted Comfort, who is only five years older than me, inspired me to lift weights and play football. A graduate of Harvard University, Ted was instrumental in my working at Silver Gold Beach Club and various other jobs I had growing up.

My teacher in high school, Mr. Dick Web, to whom I lost a bet in shop class—he actually cut my hair in class and then took me to a barber who couldn't fix it, so I ended up with a shaved head. Thanks too to Mr. Cohen, Mr. Miller, and Coach Jack Kershman, who also shared their passion for life and football with me.

My maternal grandfather, Bill Botwinik, who was always there with wisdom and money whether I asked for them or not. He would call and inspire me, send me newspapers articles and books, and lectured me every day.

My brothers, Robert and John. God knows the three of us were born very different! My younger brothers have supported my decisions and have always been there to pump me up.

My grandmother, Hennie, who lived in the Bronx, New York, would force my brothers and me to eat even after we finished a meal.

Dorothy and Benson Schussler, my aunt and uncle, were always there for me.

My cousins Martha and Frank Valladares and Sam and Norman Schussler played such an important part in my early years.

Jason Schussler, my nephew, son of my brother Robert, didn't quit and finished college after a long self-evaluation.

Sunhi Ryan, whose love and affection, writing skills, and patience has made my life (and the lives of my family, friends, and creative team) easier! I'm happy that I have found somebody who can handle my endless energy, multitasking, and sometimes hard-to-handle spirited personality.

Thank you, Tilman Fertitta, for having the courage and vision after buying Rainforest Cafe to invest in T-Rex and Yak & Yeti. It's one thing to invest in Rainforest Cafe, a public company that opened forty-five locations on three continents. But it's something entirely different to invest in the Schussler Creative team and two unopened, unproven new restaurant/retail concepts after seeing them in our laboratories in Minneapolis. Your bold decision has enabled us to continue our partnership. Thanks to your support, millions of families are enjoying great restaurant experiences together at Rainforest Cafe, T-Rex, and Yak & Yeti.

🍃

"Famous" Dave Anderson, whose unselfish friendship and entrepreneurial spirit helped lead others to invest in Rainforest Cafe. Leading by example, he wrote the first check for half a million dollars to support the opening of the first Rainforest Cafe at Mall of America in 1994.

Kim Anderson, who provided our company early on with fire retardant solutions to apply to our greenery so that the canopy I developed for our rainforest-themed Rainforest Cafe could pass health, fire, and building inspections. His tireless commitment to help us is appreciated and will never be forgotten.

Lyle Berman, who gave me credibility and brought the financial team together to enable me to open the first Rainforest Cafe. His friends and family shared his outlandish experiences when touring my St. Louis Park home, which had been transformed into a prototype of the Rainforest Cafe. I'm so thankful Lyle took the time to talk to my father. Without Lyle there would have been no Rainforest Cafe, no T-Rex, no Yak & Yeti, and no credibility. I've said this many times: there are men who see mountains, there are men who climb mountains, but only a few men dare move mountains; Lyle Berman is a mountain mover. When you identify with a common purpose, when you share ownership in a vision, you find yourself doing life's work instead of just doing time. Lyle, thank you for sharing the vision that made Rainforest Cafe possible.

Maribeth Bisienere, for without her T-Rex and Yak & Yeti

would not have had a chance of being introduced to the Walt Disney family. She is one of the brightest business women I've ever met, someone with whom I could work in any circumstance, in any business, for life. She's funny; a wonderfully talented, educated, and incredible communicator; a woman with the highest of values and integrity and a sense of community. Her gifts just begin there, and also include having such a great family and giving back so graciously to her community and peers.

Jeff Bornmann, whose friendship, professionalism, and camaraderie have made us a better company. He is always flexible and calming, complementing my yang with his yin. Wearing many different hats, he has demonstrated masterful skills and abilities in adapting to an ever-changing landscape.

Maxine Clark, creator and chairman of the board of Build-A-Bear, whose respect and friendship allowed us to become strategic partners in Build-A-Dino by Build-A-Bear, which today represents 50 percent of retail sales in the two T-Rex stores we've opened.

Bud Dare, whose early belief in me and in Rainforest Cafe paved the way for me to open Rainforest Cafe at Walt Disney World and therefore provided our company with the opportunity to go public. I owe a great deal to him for the method and the unending support he displayed.

On a Delta Airlines flight to Las Vegas, I met a flight attendant named Patrick Esposito. I admired his tie because it was the same color red as the one being worn by the gorilla on the cover of this book. I was posing for my author photo that week and needed a tie of the same color. After discussing this with Patrick, I asked if I could buy his tie. I asked him if it was part of his regular uniform, and he said yes. I then asked if the tie was sold in a catalog; he said he would gladly sell me his tie because he couldn't wait to take it off. The other flight attendants laughed and clapped as Patrick took off his tie and I handed him a ten-dollar bill. Thanks, Patrick.

Tom Farrell, thank you for all your hard work and great legal advice. You're a great friend.

Dennis FitzSimons, my boss at Telerep in Chicago, where I was a rep for TV stations throughout the United States. He allowed me the freedom to grow as an entrepreneur and not be pigeonholed into thinking like everyone else. Dennis is the former chairman of the board and CEO of the Tribune Broadcasting Company, which owned WGN Television and the Chicago Cubs. I learned a tremendous amount from him.

Dave Flom. What do you say about a guy who has played such an important role in all of our projects? Amazingly multitalented, he has helped with breeding birds for Rainforest Cafe, working with animatronics for T-Rex, and rebuilding motorcycles for Backfire BBQ. Thank you for your friendship, dedication, and hard work.

Steve Friedheim, my friend from Miami who died unexpectedly and too soon, encouraged me with his out-of-the-box thinking and never-accept-a-no attitude. He was so outrageous and incredibly generous. My love for tropical birds came from his interest in birds.

Jean Golden, our public relations and marketing guru, who graciously accepts change and is such a large part of our success.

Jannette Gonzales, whose tireless commitment to our team is evident in everything she does.

John Goodman, Sid Goodman and the Goodman Group, Nasser Kazeminy and the Kazeminy family, for without their love, support, and generosity we most certainly would not have achieved success in the opening of T-Rex Cafe and Yak & Yeti. They provided funds to continue when finding suitable financial partners was difficult, never asking why, writing checks, and providing us the necessary seed money to see our projects through. Friendship is not a commodity that can be bought, sold, or traded. It's one of those things that you cherish, love, and appreciate.

Kari Honoroff, who has put up with me for sixteen years—man, that's a long time—as my personal assistant, and I am proud that she has been able to handle every aspect of my life.

Marvin Karlins, for his endless hours of dedication to the book, and for the timeless energy he put into interviewing more than 150 people. He certainly has heard it all from the Steve Schussler stories he's had to endure.

Dale Kivimaki. Dale and his family provided friendship, love, camaraderie, and resources for filming and capturing countless hours of all of our various projects at our laboratories without compensation.

Dan Lowe, Steve Graham, Scott Rehorn, Jon Donohue, Brett Kroener, and the family at Red Development, whose unselfishness brought T-Rex and Backfire BBQ to The Legends at Village West in Kansas City, Kansas. Steve Graham brought a pin into my office and placed it on a map (after I told him that Kansas City was not a target market), and began a campaign to bring T-Rex to The Legends in Kansas City. Dan Lowe's fight in life is ferocious; he broke all barriers.

Former Mayor Carol Marinovich of Kansas City, Kansas, who as an educator saw T-Rex as an interactive educational tool, and as CEO of the Unified Government supported bringing

T-Rex to Kansas City, Kansas. Mayor Joe Reardon and the Unified Government in Kansas City, Kansas, took the baton and continued their incredible support and initiative to use Star Bonds to bring T-Rex and Backfire BBQ to The Legends in Kansas City. Their courage and support in the face of some difficult hurdles will always be appreciated.

Rich Melman, who as one of the world's top restaurateurs met with me endlessly during the early years of creating T-Rex Cafe. At his Arizona home, we spent countless hours thinking of ways to make T-Rex a world-class attraction, restaurant, and retail store. I am indebted to him for his time, commitment, and friendship, both to me and to Smile Network International.

Tim Myslajek, whose family and friendship I cherish. His support and that of Myslajek Accounting has been key in our planning, and he has played a key role in our success.

Ernie Pesis owned the building where Jukebox Saturday Night was located in Minneapolis, Minnesota. His and his family's friendship and support gave me the freedom and support to build a network of friendships and business associates that was such an important part in my life's journey.

Norm and Dorothy Pink, whose early financial support in Jukebox Saturday Night helped me when there were few other options.

Paul Ridgeway and the Ridgeway family, who always involved me in community events; they were responsible for putting on the World Championship Minnesota Twins ticker tape victory parade and Curt Carlson's Christmas party. Paul and his family are committed friends and taught me the real meaning of true friendship, as shown in bad times not in good.

Jimmy Rittenberg, who has saved my life on more than one

occasion; he taught me the night club business and gave me the opportunity to turn my retail store Jukebox Saturday Night into a chain of night clubs/restaurants. Before becoming a nightclub chain, Jukebox Saturday Night specialized in antique jukeboxes, slot machines, and carousel horses, and was located on Wells Street in Chicago (down the street from where John Belushi got his start). The night club chain consisted of four in Chicago; one in Des Moines; one in Springfield, Massachusetts; San Francisco; and finally one in Minneapolis, Minnesota. Jimmy, whom I call Mr. Chicago, aka the prince of fun, is someone whose friendship, guidance, and tutelage I will always respect and be grateful for.

David Siegel. During the horrific 9/11 events, David and his team at Central Florida Investments allowed us to house our dinosaurs in the exhibit I created around T-Rex in my quest to share the attraction, restaurant, and retail store with the Walt Disney World company.

Herb Simon, together with his brother Mel, the largest mall developers in the world, invested a half a million dollars in tenant allowance money after visiting my home and taking the tour of the prototype. Herb and his family are visionaries who are not afraid to invest in entrepreneurial startups. You never forget who brought you to the dance.

Mel Simon, whose phone call one day discussing his investment in an animated dinosaur company led me on the quest to create T-Rex, a Prehistoric Family Adventure, a Place to Eat, Shop, Explore, and Discover.

Brian Stone, from whom I learned such a great deal. We met at Vic Tanney gym, lifted weights together, ate steak tidbits, and had some cocktails. We became roommates, living in a penthouse together in Miami Beach, and I was fortunate enough to be best man at his wedding. His friendship and the interactions I had with him, his friends, and his family led me on my quest to be in the radio and broadcasting industry.

Rick Turnquist. Rick helped a great deal during the early years of Rainforest Cafe. He worked with tropical birds, and also had a great command of the English language and was a walking spelling champion and a virtual encyclopedia. Thanks for all the help with the creation of Rainforest Cafe and for being a lifelong friend.

Tom Zappia is a world-class attorney, a great family man, and a great friend. During a difficult time, he held up billing me for two years and continued working on my business with as much enthusiasm and attention to detail as he would give much larger paying clients.

The team at Schussler Creative: the term *team* takes on a whole new meaning when you think about the camaraderie and the escapades that we create on a daily basis. I cherish the time and the individual sacrifices that have been made by all of those with whom we work every day and those with whom we've come in contact over the years. Thank you for your undying support and loyalty.

I would like to thank all of the unsung heroes who have not been named but have touched our lives and influenced us every day, the UPS and Federal Express drivers and mailmen; the sanitation workers, police and firemen; city, county, and federal government employees we interact with; the secretaries, executives, receptionists, truck drivers, and delivery people; and all of the professors and college students we speak with. Thank you for having influenced our lives and for having been part of our success.

A book of this type could not be written without the generous assistance and insights of dozens—actually, more than a hundred—helpful individuals. For the sake of brevity and fairness, we have included the names of these individuals in alphabetical order below. If we have inadvertently left some names off the list, we deeply regret the oversight. To those of you whose names follow, thank you for all you have contributed to this project. We couldn't have done it without you!

Susan Abramowitz, Cindy Abramovitz, George Aguel, Greg Alstad, Dave Anderson, Kim Anderson, Louie Anderson, Peggy Arthur, Douglas Bach, Charleen Bacigalupo, Gregory Bailey, Mark Bartholomay, Lyle Berman, Phil Bernard, Harry Billger, Sandra Billings, Maribeth Bisienere, Iris Blasi, Elizabeth Blau, Chrissy Bloemendal, Jeff Bornmann, Joe Bortz, William Botwinik, Dr. Barbara Bowers, Bruce (Two Dogs) Bozsum, Keith Bradford, Robert Bram, Brooks Branch, Ken Brimmer, Jeff Cantwell, Greg Carey, Tate Carlson, Bud Cataldo, Wing T. Chao, Kathy Chen, "C. J.," Dave Claflin, Maxine Clark, Stephen Cohen, Mr. Cohen, Michael Cohen, Senator Norm Coleman, Ted Comfort, Scott Conant, Tim Conklin, Joel Conner, Ken Cooley, David Crabtree, Michael Crohn, Gary Crowder, Pat Cruzen, Megan Cullen, Cuningham Group, Dan Daddona, Carol Daniel, Bud Dare, Karen Daroff, Scott Darst, Michael Davies, Dayanny M. De La Cruz, Carlo Devito, Bob DiMarcantonio, Jon Donahue, Paul Douglas, Richard Dooley, Billy Ellis, Steve Engel, John Erickson, Patrick Esposito, Mitchell Grossinger Etess, Preston Evans, Thomas Farrell, Tilman Fertitta, Dennis FitzSimons, Dave Flom, Jon Flor, Ric Florell, Ann

Fontaine, Steven Frattalone, Mary Freidheim, Steve Freidheim, David and Jan Gee, Raphael Ghermezian, Jean Golden, Dr. Bob Goldman, Jannette Gonzales, John Goodman, Sid Goodman and the Goodman Group, Jon Gordon, Steve Graham, Juliet Grames, Shelley Green, Clark Griffith, Walter Griffin, Kurt Hagen, Robert Hahn, Meredith Hale, Jeffrey Hartmann, Patrick Hamelet, Don Hamlin, Kevin Hammerbeck, Karmen Kelly Hanson, Heather Harford, Joan Harrington, Penelope Haynes, Nick Hay, Dennis Hays, Amos Heilicher, James Henke, Grandmother Hennie, Doug Holod, Karl Holz, Kari Honoroff, Dan Humphreys, Skip and Lee Humphrey, Lee Iacocca, Irwin Jacobs, Shelley Jacobs, Randi Johnson, Hart Johnson, Terry Johnson, Marvin Karlins, Dan Kaufman, Nader Kazeminy, Nasser Kazeminy, Coach Jack Kershman, Roberta Rose Kirschenbaum, Cynthia Kiser-Murphey, John Kitchener, Dale Kivimaki, Jon Kramer, Jay Kreider, Brett Kroener, Maureen Kucera, Ray Kuik, Patrice Kullas, Leslie Kupchella, Rick Kupchella, Helmut Lange, Kevin Lansberry, Andy Lansing, John Laub, Dan Leonard, Don Lessem, David Letterman, Larry Levy, Paul Levy, Dan Lowe, Bill Mack, Rebecca Maines, Magical Michael Makay, Rachel Maloney, Senator Bill Maravitz, Carol Marinovich, Harvey Mackay, Jean McNeal, Bob Mecay, Richard Melman, George Meredith, Ron Meshbesher, Debrah Miceli, Elizabeth Mihaltse, Wayne Mills, Alan Miller, Mr. Miller, Warren Mitchell, Ted Mondale, Lafayette Montgomery, Bill Murray, Tim and Jan Myslajek, Myslajek LTD, Dee Nolting, Charles Nurnberg, Martin O'Dowd, Paul Omodt, Doug Olson, David Page, Gloria Palazzo, Gary Parendo, Governor Tim Pawlenty, Ernie Pesis, Ruben Perez, Megan Perritt, Jimmy Pesis, Dan Peterka, Suzi Petersen, Bryce Peterson, Joe Pine, Norm and Dorothy Pink, John Provo, Joe Puliafico, Mayor Joe Reardon, Scott Rehorn, Andy Revella,

Craig Rice, Paul Ridgeway, Roz Ridgeway, John Rimarcik, Jimmy Rittenberg, Mark Robinow, Joe Rohde, David Rockwell, Dave Rogers, Gregory Rothweiler, Carlos and Ann Rullan, Debra Ruth, Sunhi Ryan, Minneapolis Mayor R. T. Rybak, Ricardo Sanchez, Glenn Sands, Maria Elaina Santiago, Ed Sarquis, Joe Senser, Steven Scheinthal, Jim Schemel, Lyla Schemel, Ira Seret, Dorothy and Benson Schussler, John Schussler, Jules Schussler, Robert Schussler, Sam Schussler, Norm Schussler, Jason Schussler, Bill Schultz, David Schultz, Heidi Schweitzer, Mike Schweitzer, Marcia Seligman, David Shea and the Shea Architect team, Marty Sherman, David Siegel, Larry Siegel, Stacey Siegel, Martin Silverberg, Eddie Silverman, Marty Silverman, Herb Simon, Mel Simon, Tom Sklar, David Solner, Bobbie Soper, Jaye Snyder, Richard Stanek, Laura and David Starr, Rob Steinberg, Jay Stieber, David Stofcik, Brian Stone, Michael Tabman, Stan Taube, Pat Tapp, Richard Tettamant, Paul Teutul Sr., Paul Teutul Jr., Jim Theros, Charlie Theros, Isaac Tigrett, Michael Townsend, Donald Trump, Philip Turner, Rick Turnquist, Marvis Tutiah, Ercu Ucan, David and Kim Valentini, Rocco Valentino, Martha and Frank Valladares, Dean Vlahos, Jeff Wagner, Todd Walker, Richard Wallace, Joel Waller, Pat Wannarka, Ned Waters, Dick Web, Al Weiss, John Wheeler, Jeffrey Wirth, Drew Wood, Kamala Young, Tom Zappia, Sue Zelickson.

Schussler Creative, Inc. Mission Statement

Inventions, Ideas, Contraptions, and Dreams!

Schussler Creative is an innovative team that embraces imagination and creates theatrical hospitality venues, attractions, and experiences unlike any other!

Passion and imagination are two of the most powerful engines of success! At Schussler Creative, the paths of free-thinking individuals cross each other. Unusual and natural talents are used in an open forum to bring collective, creative ideas to fruition. When this occurs, opportunities arise that pave the way for phenomenal events.

The environment necessary for this to happen is simple: uncompromising standards to enhance the guests' experiences and a working atmosphere that encourages creativity.

Only those who risk going too far can possibly find out how far they can go!

The Entrepreneur's Credo

I do not choose to be a common man.

It is my right to be uncommon—if I can. I seek opportunity—not security. I do not wish to be a kept citizen, humbled and dulled by having the state look after me.

I want to take the calculated risk; to dream and to build, to fail and succeed.

I refuse to barter incentive for a dole; I prefer the challenges of life to the guaranteed existence; the thrill of fulfillment to the stale calm of Utopia.

I will not trade freedom for beneficence nor my dignity for a handout. I will never cower before any master nor bend to any threat.

It is my heritage to stand erect, proud, and unafraid; to think and act for myself; to enjoy the benefit of my creations and to face the world boldly and say: This, with God's help, I have done.

All this is what it means to be an Entrepreneur.

Adapted from "An American's Creed," an essay by Dean Alfange, which first appeared in the early 1950s.

The Artist's Credo

by Douglas Bloch

To receive the inspiration to create, to share that creation with others, and to be totally supported in the process.

An inspiration that calls us to create. Once the inspiration is received, then we can bring that vision into the world as a song, painting, book, invention, new business, or any other tangible form.

After the creation is born, it needs to be shared with others. No one creates in a vacuum. It is only when the vision is successfully communicated to its intended audience that it truly comes alive.

The artist needs to be supported for what he does. If he has made a positive connection with his audience, the support will come—financially and emotionally. While it may not always be there immediately, it will ultimately arrive. This is where the artist needs to trust and be patient.

This dream is not just the artist's dream. It is our dream as well. Through work or play, job or family, vacation or avocation, you can experience the joy of creating, sharing, and being acknowledged. Experience this creative process and you will never grow old in spirit.

Have you ever known an artist or a dreamer who "retired"?

SELECTED BIBLIOGRAPHY

David Barbour, "Dining with Dinosaurs—T-Rex Aims to Be the Next Big Thing in Themed Restaurants." *Lighting and Sound America*, November 2006, Volume 3, Issue 12, 64–69.

Lyle Berman & Marvin Karlins, *I'm All In*. New York: Las Vegas: Cardoza Publishing, 2005.

Ira Blumenthal, *Ready, Blame, Fire*. Glendale, Ca: Griffin Publishing Group, 1998.

Erik Calonius, "America's Secret Weapon: the Garage." *Fortune*, March 4, 1996, 150–60.

Luci Cason, "How Schussler Creative Maintains Its 'Wow' Factor—Creativity Is the Engine for Success." *Restaurant Facility Business*, December 2006/January 2007, 14–18.

Mary Boltz Chapman, "The Age of Dinosaurs—Steven Schussler's T-Rex Hopes to Transport Guests to Prehistoric Times." *Chain Leader*, August 2004, 24.

Sascha Brodsky, "Once Bitten—T-Rex Is What's Next for Rainforest Café Founder Steven Schussler." *Shopping Centers Today*, June 1, 2005, 33.

Jonathan Cooper, "Red Development Inks Restaurant Partnership Deal." *The Business Journal*, Phoenix, Arizona, May 18, 2007.

Dave Elmstrom, "Will Rainforest Reign? Despite Rapid Growth Plans, One of the Hottest Stocks Around Just Might Flourish." *Twin Cities Business Monthly*, January 1998, 32–35.

Beth Ewen, "Lessons Learned—Three CEOs Tell How They're Building Their Companies." *Upsize Magazine,* June–July 2007, 58–61.

Beth Ewen, "Rainforest Café Founder Rolls out T-Rex Chain, Shops Eight More Big Ideas." *Upsize Magazine,* November 2006, 9.

David Farkas, "Creative Habitat—Steven Schussler's T-Rex is just the beginning of the concepts coming out of his idea lab." *Chain Leader,* July 2006, Online Exclusive, http://www.chainleader.com.

Michael Fickes, "All or Nothing at the Rainforest Café." *Retail Store Image,* March 1995, 44–51.

Susan Fishman, "Restaurant Think Tank—Rainforest Café Founder Tweaks Seven New Theatrical Food Concepts." *Shopping Center Business,* May 2005, 286.

Susan Fishman & Chris Thorn, "Dining with Dinosaurs." *The Midwest's Real Estate Source,* May 2005, Volume 3, Issue 9.

Forbes, "Schussler Creative and RED Development Join Forces to Create New Attractions, Themed Restaurants, Hospitality and Shopping Venues," May 18, 2007. http://www.forbes.com/businesswire/feeds/businesswire/2007/05/18/businesswire2007 0518005162r1.html.

Ellen Gabler, "Rainforest Founder Plots Big Return." *Twin Cities Business Journal,* January 14, 2005, 1.

David Gee, "Steven Schussler's Themed Restaurants Are Hot, Even in a Cold Economy." *Minnesota Business,* December 2008, 36–41.

George Gendron, "The Most Original—and Expensive—Business Card in America." *Inc.,* July 1986, 6.

Laurie Heavey, "Owner's Mental Attitude Ensures Potential of '50s Club Franchise." *Night Club & Bar,* April 1985, 16–18.

Marvin Karlins, *Romancing the Clock.* 2nd ed. Englewood Cliffs, NJ: *Prentice-Hall,* 2009.

Bob Krummert, "Will T-REX Devour K.C.?" *Restaurant Hospitality*, October 2006, 15–16.

Paul Levy, "The Man Who Makes Things Spin in Juke Box Saturday Night." *Minneapolis Star & Tribune—Sunday Magazine*, February 8, 1987, 6–12.

Steve Marsh, "Crazy as a Tyrannosaur." *Minneapolis St. Paul*, April, 2006, 105.

Matt McKinney, "Schussler Has More Themed Attractions in Store." *Minneapolis Star Tribune*, September 29, 2007.

Peter McWilliams, *You Can't Afford the Luxury of a Negative Thought*. Los Angeles: Prelude Press, 1997.

Bob Mervine, "Dining with Dinosaurs at Disney—New Themed Restaurant Signals a Makeover for Pleasure Island." *Orlando Business Journal*, March 2006, 61.

Elizabeth Millard, "Stream of Consciousness." *Minnesota Business*, December 2006, 8.

Joe Navarro & Marvin Karlins, *What Every BODY Is Saying*. New York: HarperCollins, 2008.

Nation's Restaurant News, "Schussler Creative and RED Development to Roll out Eatertainment," Concepts Section, May 18, 2007.

Maya Norris, "Road Warrior." *Chain Leader*, January 2007, 54.

Lindsey Nodgaard, "Rainforest Café Founder Gives Lecture." *Manitou Messenger*, April 11, 2003, A1.

Orlando Business Journal, "New Restaurant Concept Fits Orlando to a T," *Orlando Business Journal*, June 17–23, 2005.

Norman Vincent Peale, *The Power of Positive Thinking*. New York: Fawcett World Library, Crest Book, 1966.

Prehistoric Times, "T-Rex: An Interview with the Creator—Steve Schussler," April/May 2006, Number 77, 53.

Reilley, Mike, "An Old and New Dining Experience at T-Rex." *Orlando Attractions Magazine*, December 2008, 38–41.

Restaurant Business, "Juke Box Saturday Night," July 20, 1985, 134.

Rob Roberts, "Retail Developers Play Show and Sell." *Kansas City Business Journal*, October 15–21, 2004, Vol. 23, No. 5.

Ron Ruggles, "Concept Innovator Schussler Inks $100M Development Deal." *Nation's Restaurant News*, May 28, 2007, 8.

Patrick Sauer, "Top of the Food Chain." *Success*, November/December 2006, Volume 16, Number 8, 69–71.

Shopping Center Business, "Schussler Creative and RED Development for Partnership," July 2007.

Joyce Smith & Mark Wiebe, "Breaking Ground for the Future." *The Kansas City Star Newspaper*, October 13, 2004, Business Section.

Ronald J. Smith. "Juke Box Sat. Night: Steve Schussler's Dream Come True." *Entrepreneur*, March 1985, 32–36.

Success, "Great Comebacks: Dogged Pursuit," July/August 1987, 35–36.

Carol Tice, "Hear Him Roar: Rainforest Cafe Founder's Entrepreneurial Adventures." *Entrepreneur*, February 2007, 20.

John Vomhof, "Schussler Creative Plans Multi-Restaurant Rollout." *Minneapolis/St. Paul Business Journal*, May 18, 2007.

ABOUT THE AUTHOR

Steven Schussler is founder and CEO of Schussler Creative, Inc., a company that creates theatrical environments for attractions, restaurants, and retail stores worldwide. Recognized by *Entrepreneur Magazine* as one of the top one hundred entrepreneurs in the country, Mr. Schussler is the creator of the Rainforest Cafe, which holds the record as the top-grossing restaurant concept in the United States and, in addition, is the only restaurant in the world to be featured in every Disney theme park. In 1998 and 1999 Schussler's organization was named one of the one hundred fastest-growing companies in the country by *Fortune* magazine. In 2006, Schussler launched a chain of dinosaur-themed restaurants called T-Rex: A Prehistoric Family Adventure, A Place to Eat, Shop, Explore and Discover. The newest T-Rex—a thirty-million-dollar, thirty-thousand-square-foot establishment—opened in October of 2008 in Downtown Disney (Orlando), marking the first time that four Schussler-created restaurants were in operation at one Disney location (two Rainforest Cafes, T-Rex, and Yak & Yeti, an Asian-themed restaurant).

In addition to Rainforest Cafe and T-Rex, Schussler and his creative team continue to develop, market, and build different themed restaurants, including the newly opened Hot Dog Hall of Fame; Galaxy Drive-in; Betty & Joe's Baker and Coffee Maker; Pizza Market; and Backfire BBQ, featuring Orange County Choppers, highlighting Paul Teutul, his sons, and décor in the style of their hit TV show, *American Choppers*. Slated to open in 2011 is another Disney-located restaurant, Mahogany Boats and Ice Cream Floats, and a jazz-themed eatery, Aerobleu, in Las

Vegas's New York, New York Hotel and Casino. (A description, including photos, of these and other Schussler themed-restaurant concepts can be found at www.schusslercreative.com.) To help in expanding the company's operations, he recently partnered with Landry's and separately with RED Development (a $100 million dollar deal) to open themed restaurant attractions in retail centers throughout the United States and abroad.

Mr. Schussler has worked with several charitable and civic organizations including the Leukemia Society, the American Lung Association, and the Special Olympics. His favorite charitable organization is Smile Network International, where he advises on the board of directors and helps coordinate surgical missions to developing countries where children receive reconstructive facial surgery free of charge.

INDEX